Reina is living proof of the insigl  managing to integrate joy and unbending strength.

    —Chuck Smith Jr., Author oi *..... ...., innovative Ministry in Popular Culture.*

In this bold book, Reina Rose brilliantly conquers contemporary complexity with a mixture of rhapsodic prose and compelling moral clarity. It provides a sure life-improving roadmap and it projects buoyancy and hope while reflecting, with optical precision, the spontaneous surgings of the human soul. Well done Reina, I'm proud to know you!

    —Rabbi Daniel Lapin, author of *Thou Shall Prosper* and president of the American Alliance of Jews and Christians.

SIN TASTES GOOD

Nourishing Your Soul in an Empty Calorie World

Reina Rose

May you be filled with wisdom and live life more & more abundantly every day you live!

Love,

Reina

Sin Tastes Good

Nourishing Your Soul in an Empty Calorie World

Reina Rose

© Copyright 2020, Crown Creativity LLC. All Rights Reserved.

ISBN: 978-1-950721-13-9

Published by Crown Creativity LLC

Dedication

For my brother, with whom growing up was like heaven on earth and whose presence in heaven has given me strength beyond what I could have possibly imagined.

Acknowledgments

A special thank you to Chuck Smith Jr. for your spiritual direction, friendship, and mentorship. Our conversations together always leave me wiser and with insights for how to become more so. Thank you to my editor Lindsay Hathaway for your helpful insights and for keeping the "Christianese" out of my writing. Thank you to all my early readers for your input and encouragement. And thank you to all my friends and family—without you, I would not be the woman I am today.

Dear Reader,

I prayed for you.

Every time I sat down to write this book, I prayed for you. I prayed that what I wrote would help you start to transform your own life for the better.

If the imperfect followers of a perfect God have run you off in the past, I am truly sorry for the way you've been hurt. I pray you're still able to read this book with an open mind and an open heart.

If you used to have a relationship with Jesus but walked away from Him years ago, I pray you will start to get back in touch.

If you have a close relationship with Jesus now and actively try to follow His teachings in your life, I pray you get to know Him on an even deeper level and start to examine parts of your faith that you've never considered.

If you've never heard of the more abundant life taught in the ancient biblical Scriptures, I pray you start to get curious. But most of all, I pray you understand how truly loved you are right now—just as you are.

No matter where you may be in your spiritual journey, I pray you will discover an awareness that connects body, mind, and spirit and that brings simplicity and fulfillment into your life and the lives of those around you. As you read on, may these words serve as a catalyst for furthering that journey of the soul.

—Reina Rose

Prologue

The Four Wives Tibetan Parable

Once upon a time, a rich king had four wives.

He loved the fourth wife the most, adorned her with rich robes, and treated her to the finest of delicacies. He gave her nothing but the best.

He also loved the third wife very much and was always showing her off to neighboring kingdoms. However, he feared that one day she would leave him for another.

He also loved his second wife. She was his confidante and was always kind, considerate, and patient with him. Whenever the king faced a problem, he could confide in her, and she would help him get through the difficult times.

The king's first wife was a very loyal partner and had greatly contributed in maintaining his wealth and kingdom. But he didn't love her. Although she loved him deeply, he hardly noticed her.

One day, the king fell ill, and he knew his time was short. He thought of his luxurious life and wondered, *I now have four wives with me, but when I die, I'll be all alone.*

Thus, he turned to his fourth wife saying, "I have loved you the most, endowed you with the finest clothing, and showered great care over you. Now that I'm dying, will you follow me and keep me company?"

"No way!" she replied and walked away without another word. Her answer cut like a sharp knife right into his heart.

The sad king then asked his third wife, "I have loved you all my life. Now that I'm dying, will you follow me and keep me company?"

"No!" replied the third wife. "Life is too good! When you die, I'm going to remarry!" His heart sank and turned cold.

He then turned to his second wife asking, "I have always turned to you for help and you've always been there for me. When I die, will you follow me and keep me company?"

"I'm sorry, I can't help you out this time!" she replied. "At the very most, I can only send you to your grave."

Her answer came like a bolt of lightning, and the king was devastated.

Then a voice called out, "I'll leave with you and follow you no matter where you go."

The king looked up and saw his first wife. She was so skinny, suffering from malnutrition. Greatly grieved, the king said, "I should have taken much better care of you when I had the chance!"

The fourth wife is our body.

No matter how much time and effort we lavish in making it look good, it will leave us when we die.

The third wife is our possessions, status, and wealth.

When we die, it will all go to others.

The second wife is our family and friends.

No matter how much they have been there for us, the furthest they can stay by us is up to the grave.

And the first wife is our soul, often neglected in pursuit of wealth, power, and pleasures of the ego.

However, our soul is the only thing that will follow us wherever we go.

So, cultivate, strengthen, and cherish it now, it is your greatest gift to offer the world.

A Note on Language

In this book, I refer to many topics using terms from biblical texts. I use words like *sin, soul, mercy, grace, God, Jesus,* and *Christ.* If these terms don't resonate the same for you, I invite you to use whatever words that will help you connect to the Source of all creation so you can draw deeper into a place of peace.

As a fitness professional for over a decade and a student of theology for much longer than that, I will be drawing comparisons between bodily fitness and soul health. I hope this analogy will help you draw your own connections between the intangible soul that our culture tends to misunderstand and the tangible body that we understand quite well.

For the record, the comparison of spiritual and bodily nutrition is not something I invented and is certainly nothing new. The Bible compared bodily nutrition to spiritual nourishment millennia ago when it called its readers to be full of the *fruits of the spirit* (love, joy, peace, patience, kindness, goodness, faithfulness, gentleness, and self-control). If only we were all full of this kind of spiritual nutrition.

Unless otherwise noted, all Bible verses are quoted from the New American Standard Bible translation.

Contents

"Folly is a joy to him who lacks sense."

—Proverbs 15:21

Why does doing the wrong thing sometimes just seem to feel so right? Why does the temptation to be a bit naughty sound quite nice? What is it about dating the bad boy or living life on the edge that can feel so exciting? Are our brains just programed to push the envelope and crave the exotic and off-limits, as long as we don't get our hands caught in the cookie jar?

Lessons in Personal Training

Buns of Steel was my favorite movie growing up. What's that—*Not a movie*, you say? Try telling that to this seven-year-old. Is it any surprise I grew up to become a personal trainer and Pilates instructor for more than ten years?

Making fitness fun for people who otherwise found it quite a chore became my greatest joy. I loved to point them in the right nutritional direction, keeping them accountable for their fitness-related choices in and out of the gym, and making it so much fun that they actually wanted to come back.

I cheered on my clients as they sculpted six packs, transformed from stick figures to hourglass shapes, or banded together as families to all lose weight. But outside appearances weren't what I found most fulfilling. It was the inner work I saw take root: the strength, flexibility, energy, and zeal that come when we start treating our bodies like temples. People finally touching their toes for the first time in their lives. Ninety-year-old women stretching their arms above their heads to reach dishes in the cupboard. And other capabilities we so easily take for granted.

I hope this book can be something like a personal trainer for the soul. And while I may not be able to do the work for you, maybe we can make the training something different…maybe even enjoyable.

Working with people from so many walks of life made me realize how fortunate mine is. As a white girl raised in a Christian family

1

in an affluent part of California in one of the most privileged nations in the world, my life can look pretty perfect from the outside looking in. But looks can be deceiving, just as someone can look good on the outside and still be incredibly unhealthy within.

I write about many of the things in this book because I've struggled with them all my life. I have learned that pride surely does come before a fall, and it's entirely possible that if I were to lose sight of that for a moment, I'd likely fall right back into my old, destructive ways.

Most people look at personal trainers like we've never eaten a cookie. But *oh, we do.* I remember an old colleague telling me that he constantly worried a client would see him whenever he drove through a fast-food window. I'll be upfront right here and right now: I still go through the spiritual drive through from time to time.

I write from a place of healed brokenness, not perfection. And I hope that sharing how I have healed will help others to heal, as well. As one who has fallen into this world's pitfalls time and time again, I want to place a few warning signs for anyone traveling behind me.

So, here are the marks and scars of my own soul. Here's what those scars have taught me, and here's hoping you will choose a better path.

We're Going to Fail

I saw three types of people in my time as a personal trainer. Some stuck to our training plans religiously. Others fell off the wagon and got back on. Plenty stumbled and never came back. I pointed my clients toward professionals who could help them create healthy nutrition plans to not just look fit but also feel full of energy. When they followed the plan, they looked and felt amazing. But old habits die hard. One slice of cake would lead to another, and sometimes they'd gain more weight than they had when we started. Once they acknowledged the challenge, they'd get right back to working toward health again.

The further we get from the ideal way of living, the further we get from our ideal way of looking and feeling. Though living in wise

2

ways is a large part of it, there's no benefit to pointing moralistic fingers to tell people how they should live.

There's no "calories in/calories out" formula to follow to maintain a healthy soul. But God did give us a nutrition plan. Biblical scripture tells the story of a historical figure called Emmanuel (*God with us*) who's basically the ultimate soul trainer. It's time we dig into these ancient teachings for ourselves.

If you're completely turned off by Christianity because of judgmental so-called followers of Jesus, you're not alone. Even the best trainer has some problem clients. But even if you fall off the soul train altogether, are you determined to stick around or cut and run the moment you break a sweat?

Missing the Mark Again

This is a big one, so pay attention.

Sin. Depending on your religious background (or lack thereof), the word might make you cringe, become immediately defensive, or mean nothing to you at all. But all the word *sin* really means is to miss the mark.

Have you ever tried archery? Maybe at camp as a kid? If so, you know how easy it can seem to set that bull's-eye in your sight only to shoot the arrow and watch it veer miserably off the course you thought you'd set. No one would call that kid a failure; they just need more practice.

How often do we miss the mark in life? For most of us, there is a gap between what we have become and what we would like to be—not to mention all we are created for. Most of us would like to close that gap and walk a few feet closer to the bull's-eye, yet few of us know how or even what the target is. Maybe the target is heaven on earth—the figurative Eden, a promised land that God intended for our lives and left a road map to reach.

Many of today's Bible scholars refer to a biblical event they call *the fall* or *original sin,* when the first humans disobeyed the boundaries God set for them and could no longer remain in paradise. Reflecting on this story of Adam and Eve walking side by side in a garden of perfection, striking up conversations with their Creator, eating all they

3

want and still looking great naked, we might pause to ask ourselves what possessed them to desire anything different? What seemed to promise *more* than perfection?

Put aside any questions of whether this ancient allegory is literal or figurative for a moment to focus on the overarching lesson: Even when given a state of perfection, humans seem to have a propensity to wander into the forbidden, to things that ultimately lead to far less than the perfection we were created for. Unsurprisingly, the story's characters do not fare well after eating the forbidden fruit.

The consequence for this action is that they must leave the garden, start wearing clothes, and work hard for their food. No thanks! Who in their right mind would trade living in a lush garden and enjoying delicious food while chatting it up with The Most Interesting Being in the Entire Universe?

But that's just the thing. Our characters could never have possibly imagined the consequences of such a simple and seemingly innocent decision as they stared into the shining surface of the beautiful fruit that is described as "pleasing to the eye and filled with promise for more." As temptation whispered about its wonderful taste, ability to open the mind, and desirability for others, they never could have fathomed how drastically life would change for the worse shortly after enjoying this seemingly simple pleasure.

Sin looks good and often tastes good—addictively so. So, what should we do about it? Sin draws us in, takes us further than we wanted to go, and promises more than it ever gives. Even knowing this, we seem to keep falling into the same old traps. It's like knowing you will eat the gallon of ice cream in one sitting and get the bellyache of the century...yet buying it anyway!

But what if we could recognize these temptations? To see how they keep tricking us into thinking there is something better out there than God's plan for us. How many stories have we heard of people leaving their spouses for what promised to be more, give more, and provide more, only to end up alone and working harder than they ever imagined to hold together a broken family that their passionate, momentary choices split apart? How often do we wake up from the sting of a wild night out, our bodies protesting never to do *that* again,

4

only to hit repeat the following weekend, encouraging our friends to come with? How many people finally get the success, money, or power they have been climbing toward and craving, only to discover that it doesn't fulfill as promised?

I love Jim Carey's quote on the subject: "I think everybody should get rich and famous and do everything they ever dreamed of so they can see that it's not the answer."

So, What Is the Answer?

Do the fire and brimstone preachers have the answer? Or the yogis? Maybe the New Age movement? What about the prosperity gospel? With so many people proclaiming to have found the secret to personal fulfillment, who do we believe? Where are we supposed to search for abundant living? Is the meaning of life pain or bliss, hard work or detachment?

The thing is: There is some truth in most of these belief systems, and some of these beliefs are often stepping-stones to discovering greater truth and fulfillment. Oftentimes, once we have tried all of the complex ways to accomplish something, we will discover that the simplest way was the best to begin with. Without trying all the others, however, many of us could never see the simple perfection in the simple and perfect way. We are human and have an eye for the alluring, even when it may obscure or even obliterate the good and simple things that were ours all along.

I have seen and done this many times in the areas of diet and exercise. With so many methods available for anyone willing to start, I have seen the yo-yo effects of differing food and exercise beliefs countless times. Some of these ideas are better than others, and most of them will work on some level without doing much or any physical harm to the participant. But (yo-yo dieting's mental and emotional harm not withstanding) sometimes these routines simply serve as a catalyst for bringing enough body awareness to help a person naturally discover what does and does not serve their own body: what nourishes, what fulfills, and what makes them look and feel great.

In my experience, I have seen that it is best to develop greater awareness of our own bodies in order to nourish and exercise them in the manner they need. For some, it takes trying all the wrong ways to finally find the right one, while others are able to start with a better way from the beginning. We are all on a journey. We all desire to grow to higher, wiser, more fulfilling states of living on that journey. We all start from different places, and our roads will look drastically different. But I believe that the best place to begin a journey to physical and spiritual health and wellbeing is to first develop greater awareness of our own choices, habits, and thoughts.

We see in this story that sin promises so much, but it doesn't hold up its end of the bargain. Missing the mark and continuing to allow our aim to veer off course leads beyond just unfulfillment. Our figurative arrows can hurt others, hurt ourselves, and ultimately bring all kinds of destruction and unhappiness that just a bit of course-correction could have prevented. Come take this journey with me, and let's learn how to improve our aim together.

Sin Tasted Good

The forbidden fruit was delicious. For a while. Our addictions feel good, until they hurt. The things that we seek to satisfy our cravings often do so, until we feel the unwanted consequences of what we've done.

Why do we seek these things in the first place? It's not as if most of us haven't been warned when our choices are unwise. Some people may not have parents to teach them right from wrong, others had parents who took the "do as I say, not as I do" approach (teaching some very unwise habits to their offspring in the process), and still others had no one to guide them at all. The majority of us, however, simply choose to do the wrong things despite being warned against it—perhaps, at times, *because* we were told not to.

Proverbs 9 describes the woman of folly who proclaims that "stolen water is sweet; food eaten in secret is delicious." There is something that lures us into things we're told not to do. There's something that seems fun and exciting about being a person of folly, especially in a culture that tends to encourage and celebrate it. But the further we get from what we were meant to do and who we were meant to be, the further we get from the pleasures we are seeking. By wisdom, however, we find true and lasting pleasure. It is by wisdom that we not only experience pleasures in body and spirit, but also know how to savor and enjoy them.

There is One who created humans and knows our nature. As a good parent guides their children not to run in busy streets or stick forks in electrical sockets, our Creator laid out guidelines to help. God's will is to keep His children safe, protected, and flourishing. It is our free will to choose this protection and wisdom or to neglect it. God gives us that choice, even if we break His heart by intentionally choosing things we know are foolish. If children decide to stick the fork in the socket or run out in the street despite their parents' warnings, they're likely to get hurt. And when we choose to reject wisdom and do whatever feels right in the moment, we'll likely get hurt, too.

This is true for many things in life. Things that God set up to be wonderful human experiences under the correct boundaries have become excursions into playing spiritual *Frogger* with our souls. The further we get from the wise and perfect design, the further we roam from a truly satisfying life into an open road of speeding harm.

Developing Consciousness

Most people realize that coupling physical activity with certain types of foods will generate a certain outcome. More than ever, people are eating organic foods, exercising regularly, and even doing some form of moving meditation. What I find mind-boggling is that, as a culture, we tend to feed our souls the spiritual equivalent of fast food and donuts and then wonder why we feel more apathetic, depressed, and anxious than ever. We feed our souls large amounts of debt, meaningless sex partners, drugs, and alcohol just to name a few. We try to satiate our human needs without the greater need of actual companionship. We seek enlightenment by using bottle, needle, or pill to subvert consciousness. But the true test of all these mechanisms might be how we really feel when they are gone. Do they truly satisfy?

Or do they only leave us wanting another purchase, another partner, or another hit? Truly, these behaviors are like eating another liter of ice cream to solve the problem of feeling fat.

Health-conscious people are starting to search beyond solutions for their problems to what caused the problems in the first place. Perhaps a headache is a sign of needing to hydrate or a stomachache is begging us to eat less acidic foods. But what about sadness? What about anger? What about the emotional feelings that we wish to block or numb? There are drugs to numb those, too. But as spiritually health-conscious people, could we search for the root causes of these feelings? Or have we become so used to emotionally burying our heads in the sand that we would rather run than address them? Would we rather pop a pill than admit to ourselves that the cheesy pizzas and sodas we feed our souls may be giving us spiritual heartburn?

Donuts and the Meaning of Life

I used to love donuts. They always looked like they were going to taste amazing. But for well over a decade, every time I actually ate a donut, I'd feel incredibly sick to my stomach within minutes. My stomach would rumble so loudly that it sounded like some horrible creature was going to crawl out like a scene from *Alien* (or *Spaceballs*). I'd start looking around for the nearest bathroom signs, wondering how in the world I fell into that sugar grease trap once again. Even now, I still have to remind myself that, regardless of how promising those beautiful pastries look, they are *not* my friends.

I believe certain life choices can be much like donuts. In hindsight, some choices look so enticing only to leave us doubled over in pain. This purchase will make me feel great—that shot of dopamine rushing through my veins into my brain said so. But if buyer's remorse doesn't set in right away, how long before the overdue credit card bill shows up on the doorstep? How long before the feelings of loneliness creep back in after a meaningless hookup? Will nagging thoughts about possible STD or pregnancy have subsided before they do? Will the hangover, bags under the eyes, and premature aging be worth those barely remembered nights out? Will being the most successful person you know really make you happy at the end of the day?

The answers to these questions may be different for everyone, but we have to be aware enough to even ask them in the first place. I hope this book helps you start asking yourself the right questions about yourself. Let's become aware of the ways we live and ask ourselves if the paths we're on are heading in the directions we want to go? If not, what must we do to change them?

Do we want financial stability? Will our current earning and spending habits take us there? Do we want loving relationships with people we can count on and joyfully grow old with? Do we want to be completely aware of our surroundings when we have fun and be able to remember the experience, engage in meaningful conversations along the way, and forge relationships that grow stronger over the years with people we respect and admire? How do we start making those changes when we decide we want them?

I've heard it said that we are the sum total of the questions we ask ourselves. I think we're a bit more than that, but I do believe asking questions is a great start to developing consciousness. It's easy to point the finger at *them* (whoever *they* are) and refuse to acknowledge the part we play in a culture that we believe has gone amiss. Awareness of the role we play in our own lives is the first step toward bringing change to the world around us. We must have awareness of our souls.

How To Read This Book

I set up this book in a way that I hope will make it easy for you to reflect as you read. Each chapter is filled with smaller sections broken into short, digestible soul snacks. Consider it like a multi-course gourmet meal to be savored, rather than fast food that'll give you a full stomach with little to no nutritional value.

Food for Thought

At the end of each entry, you will see a series of questions. Think on them alone with a notebook or together in a group of friends. Take a few minutes of contemplation to consider these prompts before moving on to the next entry.

Selah

The word *Selah* is used more in the Hebrew Scriptures than both *amen* and *hallelujah* combined. It's used as a musical interlude as a time for pause and reflection and is thought to be rooted in the Hebrew word *Selal*, which is translated to *build up, lift up, or exalt*. At the end of each entry, I invite you to sit quietly in the rest and reflection of *Selah*. And if you just can't put it down, please feel free to read the whole book through, coming back to spend time in quiet contemplation as you read it again and again.

PART 1:
Discovering Your Inner Soul

What is the soul? Philosophers, theologians, and scientists have always puzzled over this question. It's not scientifically measurable or tangibly quantifiable, so even its existence is up for debate. But general consensus considers the soul to be the source of our very existence and individuality. Whether attributing all aspects of the soul to behaviorism, social conditioning, or something more mystical, the soul is a vital part of who we are. In simplified Christian terms, our souls are the purest part of our beings, often referred to as our true selves made in the image of God.

Show Me Your Soul

"I think I fall in love a little bit with anyone who shows me their soul. This world is so guarded and fearful. I appreciate rawness so much."

—Emery Allen, writer

Think of someone who has shown you their soul—someone willing to be vulnerable enough to humbly and truthfully reveal the good, bad, and ugly parts of themselves, without complaining or seeking sympathy. How easy was it for you to connect with them? Chances are their openness probably made you feel so comfortable and accepted that you opened up about your own life, revealing your own soul and connecting with each other in true intimacy.

Now think about the people who've only shown you the beautiful, successful parts of themselves. They tend to seem untouchable: superhuman and unrelatable at best, arrogant and unwelcoming at worst. It's often difficult to be vulnerable with these people, feeling insignificant next to such supposed demigods—like posting about your boring day in an endless feed of top social media influencers.

I used to be the second type of person: obsessed with portraying happiness at all times and priding myself in always being equipped with the perfect advice or positivity-focused mantra for anyone who'd dare show the slightest grey cloud on their mental horizon. I was all sunshine and rainbows—*only*—don't you dare rain on my parade. Eventually, it took a personal apocalypse-level storm to see what I was doing wrong.

Sure, I could bring positivity and motivation to the direst of circumstances, but I completely lacked empathy. I couldn't relate or listen when someone needed to process difficult emotions, let alone simply share any real, honest parts of their lives. I even formed a positivity group called the Happy Women's Society, only inviting people I knew would never sit around complaining about their lives (as I believed most of the world was prone to doing). How obnoxious. Most of our meetings were upbeat, often centered on some motivational book recommendation. Some members would read, some wouldn't, and I did my best not to place any expectations beyond maintaining that constant optimism I considered essential to the surreally unrealistic cocoon that held our group connection.

Light Shines Through the Cracks

Then, at just twenty-four years old, my brother—my best friend in the whole world—died suddenly in a motorcycle accident. We were the kind of siblings who did everything together, from weekly Disneyland trips to regular music sessions at each other's houses. Suddenly he was gone, and so was I. I stopped eating and quickly become gaunt and disheveled, with eyes that carried the hollow look of someone who's died alongside her loved one. I was a mess, a shell of the vibrant girl everyone knew. Very few people saw me during that dark time, and those who did almost always expressed deep concern.

Meeting for the first time since the crash, one friend from the positivity group said something that's always stayed with me. She told me that seeing me after my brother died was the first time she had actually been able to see me as human, as relatable. She saw my vulnerability and finally felt like she could be vulnerable with me.

I was completely shocked. Didn't she see all the Pinterest quote-style positivity I'd plastered all over my life? Was I just a cliché?

Over the next couple of weeks, I thought about how little I had my life together and how vulnerable I had always been inside, even before my brother's passing. Sure, I had so much to be grateful for, but the image of success that I had built up was mostly just my attempt at positive self-talk to "fake it till you make it" and nothing like my reality. I wanted to focus on what I wanted in life, rather than on what I didn't want. But I also wanted to be approachable, relatable, and someone with whom others could share their entire selves—not just the pretty and put-together parts. Something was changing in me; a new perspective was beginning to emerge.

Thank God those beautiful women in that misguided positivity group stuck with me and set me straight with their kindness and genuine hearts, helping me to realize how much I was completely missing the point. Now, when I see someone else portraying that same happy veneer or spouting some happiness cliché, I remind myself to pause my judgment and show a little compassion because it wasn't so long ago that that person was me.

True or False?

I think a lot about what Trappist monk and theologian Thomas Merton has said about the true and false self. The *true self*, he says, is the soul—the true essence of what God has created us to be—while the ego displays the *false self* or how we'd like to be seen. Back when my friend thought I was bulletproof, I was living behind a self-created wall of false happiness and success. What a sad, lonely place to live. It wasn't until the walls of this false self were shaken to the ground, until the image I had built was nothing but rubble at my feet, that I could begin to embrace the true beauty we are all created to live in.

And I've been happy and perfect ever since. *Just kidding.* Turns out, it takes hard work to live authentically from your soul. I'd love to say I began to live in my true self after my brother's death and have lived more and more from the depths of my soul ever since, but it's just not the case.

What I have learned, though, is that discovering my true self and breaking down my ego-driven false self is a process I must live through time and time again—prayerfully at greater levels each time. Yet the journey to first confronting my false self has led me deeper into my true self than I could have possibly known to hope for in those days, and it continues to draw me deeper still.

The journey to living in one's soul—in the true self—can be confusing at times, and yet the struggle is a good fight. It is a fight to become more real in a world that is often so fake, to strip away that which no longer serves in a world that tells us we must put on what it has to offer in order to be of value within its system. The fight toward living in truth, grace, and love helps us embrace the true beauty we were created to live in and get closer to the original design for which we were created. It's a struggle worth fighting, so let's get going.

"Ask and it will be given to you; seek and you will find; knock and the door will be opened to you. For everyone who asks receives; the one who seeks finds; and to the one who knocks, the door will be opened" (Mathew 7:7–8 NIV).

Food for Thought

- In what ways do I live in my true self? Am I vulnerable, openhearted, and approachable?
- In what ways do I still live in my false self? Do I try to live up to an image that I hope people see in me? Do I sit in stillness with the depths of my emotions, or do I tend to avoid them or cover them with affirmations until I feel a semblance of happiness?
- How can I live more in my true self and less in my false self?
- What do I think Jesus meant when He said, "If any of you wants to be my follower, you must give up your own way, take up your cross, and follow me"? (Matthew 16:24 NLT)

Selah.

14

What is the Soul?

"And the Word became flesh, and dwelt among us, and we
saw His glory, glory as of the only begotten from the Father,
full of grace and truth."

—John 1:14

The soul might be described as the part of us that is eternal, the part
that was us before we were born, and will be us after we die. I have
heard it called the *true self,* in other words, who we truly are when we
strip away all ego, social programming, and images of what we think
or want ourselves to be. My inspiration on the topic of the true self
comes from extensive writings from Thomas Merton and Richard
Rohr, which I highly recommend you check out. So, I will also be
referring to the soul as the *true self* throughout this book.

Tearing Down the False Self

If the soul actually does last so much longer than our physical bodies,
you'd think our culture would give the soul greater importance and
more value. Perhaps it's because many of us believe the soul lasts
forever that we tend to take its eternal nature for granted, neglecting it
in order to build up what the apostle Paul refers to as the *flesh* (or
false self).

   The false self is the ego-driven image of what we want to be
and how we hope to be known. Whatever you may call it, neither is
bad, and both are necessary. Many theologians and mystics say we
must come to the end of our false selves (our egos), what we think we
are and how we want to be known, before we can truly tap into our
soul, spirit, or true self. Only when the fleshly false self fails us and
neglects to bring the satisfaction we were seeking can we acknowledge
our true self and discover the joy of living from that place instead.

   What a pity if it takes coming to the end of our earthly bodies
to get in touch with our spirits! I believe that when the Bible speaks of
flesh, it's referring to the ego-driven false self. But perhaps some people
may only be able to start seeing their long-neglected true selves when
their literal flesh becomes less vital and useful.

For those of us who allow the personas we build for ourselves to get so large and in charge, there may be no other way to see our true selves than by having our built-up, dressed-up, propped-up false selves shrink to nearly nothing. It may take a near-death experience, an illness, or reaching the end of life to see our true selves and recognize the value of the soul (the part that does not die away). How sad would it be to live in a false reality until it is too late to go back and choose to live in the fullness of life throughout the entire human experience?

The Christian tradition teaches that "The Word became flesh," meaning that God incarnated and came to earth as a human. If God Himself would create a fleshly body, then come to earth in human form and personally live as Emmanuel (God with us), the simple conclusion is that bodies cannot be bad.

Bodies are necessary vessels that hold the deeper part of us, our souls. It is when we can see past the clay vessel into the content of that vessel—see the Spirit that our Creator breathed into—that we can recognize and know the soul in ourselves and others.

Revelation, inspiration, and enlightenment happen when we can be vulnerable enough to tear down the images we carefully craft to function in a society that tells us we must *be somebody*, without realizing we already are somebody created in the very image of the Most High God. This is a revelation that, if we let it, can give us the humble confidence to truly be ourselves in a world where everyone is trying to become an image they have created based on upbringing, desires, and societal expectations.

Stepping into the True Self

The greatest beauty in discovering one's true self and recognizing the inspired soul in others is that being vulnerable, humble, and kind opens up a safe space for others to reveal their own vulnerabilities and beauty of their souls. From there, true friendship (which the Greeks referred to as *Philia*) can take root. C.S. Lewis writes that "Friendship...is born at the moment when one man says to another, 'What! You too? I thought that no one but myself.'" No one can say "Me too" if they never come to know their own true selves or those around them.

Perhaps we can learn to drop the masks, see our true selves in all their beauty and recognize it in others as they take off their own masks and exclaim, "Me too!"

This is only a reminder of what your soul already knows. The nutritious intimacy that the soul craves at its deepest parts is what allows us to fully become who we really are. When we realize the many sweet, tasty empty calories that leave a bad taste in the spirit and shine a light on the nutritious aspects of a life lived in wisdom and right relationships, we are able to correct our aim and draw closer to the bull's-eye of a more abundant life.

This brings an awareness that becomes the first step toward fulfillment, revealing ancient, timeless wisdom like a recipe book for nourishing the soul and deepening relationships. When you've taken the time to deepen your own intimacy with your soul and your Creator, you embrace both the human and divine within yourself, allowing that divine breath to inspire and give you life more abundantly.

Food for Thought

- In which parts of my life do I live in my true self?
- Which parts of life reflect more of the false self-image I have created for my own satisfaction or what I want others to think of me?
- When I allow my mask to come off, how do I invite others to do the same so we can relate more authentically to each other?

Selah.

Original Good

"God saw all that He had made, and it was very good."

—Genesis 1:31, NIV

When reading a sacred text, the key is to focus primarily on the lesson being conveyed.

Many of today's Bible scholars begin the creation story in Genesis 3 with the story of Eve's temptation. But starting the story where the humans mess up completely misses the best parts, all that beauty and goodness when God breathes life into His clay creation—naked, unashamed, and modeled after Himself. Beginning at the fall and ending at redemption completely neglects the entire point of what is being redeemed. After all, you wouldn't skip the first few chapters of a book or the intro to a movie and expect to understand the full story.

In the Beginning

So, let's start the story where God began it—with original *good*, not original *sin*. God systematically declares everything He makes as good, even humans' naked bodies. The Genesis 1 poem's imagery is so heartwarming, hopeful, and caring that you can nearly feel God smiling as He creates this beautiful earth and everything in it. Soon enough, we see how humanity misses the mark (sins), with the rest of the story showing time and time again how God constantly chases after His beloved creation and offers to bring us back to closeness and intimacy with Him and each other. In an ultimate act of love, He sends His Son to show us that we must give up everything we think is important so that we may become truly alive in the goodness He has intended for us all along. Those who seek Him closely see they're clearly missing *nothing* in a world of false pretense, learning to live more like the original goodness that the Spirit of God spoke into life with His very breath.

Starting in chapter three instead of chapter one (with humans in a state of "total depravity" as John Calvin calls it), is an insult to the very Creator who formed us, then called us His own and ultimately good. When we start the Bible's story of humanity from the beginning, with the incredible gift of knowing the end, we can learn through the middle by humbly accepting the lessons that sin and failure serve to teach us. Only then can we hopefully expect to redeem the goodness we were originally created for and transform daily into God's original design, His own image.

Temptation and sin don't even enter the picture until chapter 3, when we see the half-truths of evil, symbolized by the serpent telling them how they will "be like God" (Genesis 3:5, NIV). Spinning his web of half-truths, the snake left out the very important fact that God had already made them like Him—in His image. It's not the only time we hear this lie, either. Centuries later, Jesus is fed the same half-truth when Satan tempts Him in the wilderness, ignoring Christ's divinity and pushing Him to prove He is the son of God.

Know Your Truth

Hands down, this is the biggest evil and most blatant lie that humanity has come to believe. Hook, line, and sinker, we have been convinced that the deepest and truest parts of ourselves are nothing like God. This is the exact spot where we miss the mark, forgetting this truth: that God's Spirit dwells within our human flesh.

This is where Adam and Eve ultimately went wrong, too. They weren't just mounds of clay, as evil would like them to believe, but a very mystical and beautiful mix of flesh and Spirit—the gem of God's creation. Sometimes I wonder how differently things could have gone if Adam and Eve had remembered who they were in that moment. What if, when the serpent told them eating the fruit would make them like God, they replied, *We already are like God! He made us in His very image, beautiful and alive with His own Spirit. Now get out of here!* In the same situation, Jesus later throws the mic down perfectly saying, "Away from me, Satan!" (Matthew 4:10, NIV).

The problem is that we don't always remember who we are, who made us, and the image that we model. Too many of us identify so much more with the clay than with the Spirit of God because earth and flesh are all our eyes can see. The National Eye Institute says that eighty percent of our sensory information is derived from sight, so it's no wonder we often neglect to recognize that we are also made up of spirit. It's a consistent theme in the Bible, too, as the Israelites "forget God" time and time again. They didn't literally forget that God existed, but they forgot that He intimately lived with them in loving communion. It would be like inviting a guest into your home, then never speaking to or doing anything with them. You still know they're there, but it sure doesn't seem like it. This is how the Israelites eventually treated God in their lives, how all of humanity has ultimately done throughout the ages.

The Sweet Flavor of Grace

Only one person has ever lived in true connection with humanity and divinity: Jesus, Himself. In His brief time on earth, He consistently pointed out ways that the rest of humanity also could be transformed into God's likeness as originally created. Jesus teaches us that living in the ways of the Spirit will also care for our bodies. He shows the importance of loving God and others, then teaches us a multitude of ways to do it. He shows us what humble, kind, and caring love looks like. This love is not easy or superficial, so it's no surprise that He says following Him will feel like taking up our own cross, like dying to other ways of living.

Christ teaches us that, in order to live more fully, we must die to the selfish ideas that the world revolves around us or that people are here to serve us and make us feel good. He shows us that, when we die to that part of ourselves, we will know life more abundantly and receive more than we could ever give. He calls us to be more like Him, rather than change our view of Him to become more like us.

In his book *Immortal Diamond*, Richard Rohr writes about how people are "deepening [our] relationship with a very tiny American Jesus—who happens to look an awful lot like [us]." This is what we do when we decide to live more like the clay than the Spirit, when we try to interpret scripture through the lens of our preferences rather than

20

for the purpose of seeking truth. We further call our actions "only human" or "natural" in order to justify the things we know are not right or uplifting—or worse, cover up our visible sins and pretend we have none.

I believe it's essential to know that there is more grace for our mistakes than could ever be imagined. There's simply no need to make excuses, justify, or cover them up. Just be aware of the areas in our lives where we miss the mark, seek wisdom for how to live closer to the mark that we were created to hit, and aim to live closer to the state of God's divine breath that gives us life and guides our souls into the fullest and most fulfilling ways of living. In that light, we may discover that sin does not taste so good after all. Why would we even want to eat the forbidden fruit? In fact, after getting spiritually healthier, we may discover that the sticky-sweet flavor of sin that once seemed so appealing may one day become a sour taste to our soul that we wish to avoid at all costs.

Food for Thought

- Is it easier for me to think of myself in a "state of total depravity" rather than "made in God's image?"
- In what ways does this affect my perceptions of myself and others?
- How do I behave if I think of myself as "only human" rather than a beautiful creation with the breath of God's Spirit living within me?
- How does this revelation affect the way I see those around me?

Selah.

Frozen Yogurt Fiend

"Close your mouth, block off your senses, blunt your sharpness, untie your knots, soften your glare, settle your dust. This is primal identity."

—Lao Tzu, *Tao Te Ching* classic Chinese text

One blazing hot Southern Californian day, I took a different route home from work. I had frozen yogurt on the brain, and all I could think of was stopping for a treat on my way home. *I worked hard, I deserved it, and it's healthy, right?* A few more traffic lights, and I would be there. *Would this stop light ever turn green?!* I impatiently tapped my fingers on the steering wheel, wishing the car in front of me to move, as I plotted my shortest route to frozen sugar nirvana. I could practically taste it.

Soon, I was seated on a shaded bench, lifting the golden plastic spoon to my mouth to savor the sweet goodness. The first bite melted in my mouth like always, yet something was amiss. What was it? This was my favorite dessert since I was a teenager, but when I actually stopped to taste it, I realized I didn't actually like it anymore. How could I no longer like my favorite treat? And what in the world would I reward myself with from now on?

From baklava to fudge cake, eventually my love for other sweet foods also faded. I realized I'd simply been conditioned to love all those things and consider them treats. Family, friends, and society told me they were appealing, but I didn't actually find them delicious. Now, don't get me wrong, I do still like some desserts and treat myself on occasion. But developing greater awareness of what I put in my mouth helped me learn to only eat the few sweets I actually like, instead of mindlessly consuming things that everyone else say are good. The same goes for the soul.

Frozen Yogurt for the Soul

When I really stopped to think about it, I realized this pattern of mindlessness actually permeated my entire life. I started to see it everywhere: just how unintentional and unaware I was of my thoughts and behaviors. Things like endlessly discarding plastic bottles or voicing complaints that served no real purpose…how much of life was I just mindlessly consuming and completely unaware?

No wonder my relationships suffered, my finances were out of control, and my inner world felt shockingly out of line with my outward experiences. I was missing the mark so badly that I could hardly see the target anymore. My heart wasn't in the right place. I wanted peace, love, and abundance; but I was thinking about, focusing on, and acting out of anxiety, bitterness, and desire for more. I repeated mantras of how I was always improving; but most of my words and actions were carelessly the same. The same complaining, the same blaming, the same analyzing how it could ever get any better.

Many of us have this same mentality about certain behaviors in our lives. We miss the mark because we have been programmed to think something is satisfying—a thought, word, or behavior—when it's ultimately harmful to others or ourselves. Whether because of learned behaviors from our upbringing or social conditioning, all too easily, we think things in our lives seem good, until we realize how harmful they really are for our souls.

Mindfulness Matters

It's about so much more than overindulging in meaningless desserts. Becoming aware of our focus and intention goes much deeper than the food we put into our mouths; it's about bringing awareness to the content we allow into our souls, which ultimately affects what comes out of our mouths, back into our ears, and into the consciousness of the world at large.

Think about the simple act of complaining. Complaining comes so naturally that it's even a way to bond with people who share our mutual woes. But complaining solves nothing, really; it's just keeping a negative feeling front and center in our minds, as the primary focus of our energy and words. What we focus on is ultimately what we will experience, especially when it comes to core values. If we focus on victimization, bitterness, and sadness, we will get more of the same.

Likewise, focusing on the power of our choices, forgiveness, and joy, shows us opportunities to multiply these values in our lives.

I've read about studies conducted to try to measure the power of prayer and good intention, and I'm pleasantly unsurprised at their controversial findings. For decades, doctors and hospitals have conducted tests to try to support or refute the fathomless spiritual benefits of prayer. Like cardiologist Randolph Byrd, whose 1988 study on intercessory prayer reported faster recovery rates and fewer medicinal needs for half of nearly 400 hospitalized heart patients who received anonymous prayer from afar, as opposed to the half who did not receive prayer. At the very least, studies like this show prayer's power to change our outlook.

Is it a coincidence that God's way seems to correlate with what modern research shows to cause greater success in many areas of our lives? Is it a coincidence that the modern law of attraction (manifesting positive or negative experiences through the power of thought) so closely resembles Jesus's centuries-old teachings about the power of what we believe in our hearts? Jesus takes this concept a step further, though: not just changing our words and thoughts but changing the very depths of our hearts. ("For the mouth speaks what the heart is full of."—Luke 6:45, NIV)

Food for Thought

- Am I habitually doing, thinking, or saying anything that no longer helps me or improves the world around me (or maybe never did)?
- How can I become more conscious of the ways I walk through life?
- In what ways do prayer and belief affect my daily living and the ways I impact others?

Selah.

To Sin or Not To Sin

"Therefore, if anyone is in Christ, he is a new creation. The
old has passed away; behold the new has come."

—2 Corinthians 5:7, ESV

A friend of mine has struggled with a behavioral addiction. Over the
years, she had also left her religious upbringing, then later returned to
her faith in Jesus' teachings. It was around this time that she messaged
to tell me she'd engaged in the behavior again, asking me if it was a sin
and whether she should feel bad about it.

Lord knows I've done my share of judging others over the
years, but I no longer think it's my place to tell people what I think are
their sins—and certainly not to dictate how they should feel about it.
If we are sincerely seeking truth rather than simply looking to affirm
what we want to believe, then I believe the Holy Spirit shapes our
intuition for us. So, I told her to ask God about it in prayer and pay
attention to how she felt after. Did it bring the satisfaction she
was seeking?

I believe God gives us intuition (which some Christians would
call the Holy Spirit) to know what is right and wrong for our lives. I
advised my friend to pay attention to how she felt whenever she acted
on this behavior. Did it bring the satisfaction she was seeking? Did it
feel light or heavy? I told her to pay attention to the feelings and
keep praying.

Did she do the behavior again? Yes. But this time, she said it
didn't feel right anymore, even though she thought it truly satisfied her
in the past. She decided she no longer wanted to do it.

If I'd simply told her she was wrong or sinned horribly, her
choice to continue or not wouldn't have actually been her own. And it
surely wouldn't last. But by bringing her own consciousness to the
situation through prayer and attention, she was able to come to her
own conclusions and live in a way that is in alignment with her
true beliefs.

Refining Our Tastes

If God always wants the best for us, it stands to reason that the closer we seek to follow His will, the less we will want to do anything that isn't pleasing to Him. Not because we try hard enough or have enough willpower, but because our hearts have changed. Sin no longer tastes good, as we start to crave a healthy spiritual life and recognize the difference when we're living in a way that's good for us, in the way our hearts long to live.

Like my frozen yogurt or my friend's past behavior, eventually our souls begin to notice the bitter taste sin leaves, as we realize it doesn't satiate like we thought it should. Just as making better health and fitness choices slowly transforms our former selves into healthier, happier people who eventually crave healthier food that once seemed repulsive, our spirits similarly transform as we seek God's truth. Like photos of extreme weight loss, soul transformations often look miraculous to those who know us best.

Good news: We don't need to worry about judging others or telling them how to live their lives. God will take care of that for us. And we can ease up on our own personal critiques, too.

The process of becoming a new creation (someone who seeks God's will, believing it's best for living a more abundant life) is rarely, if ever, a linear process. Much of the process toward holiness includes doubting, questioning, and feelings that have been described as "dark nights of the soul." Only God can fully know anyone's heart, so He is the only one who can truly lead us to the life He has created us to fulfill.

So, be gracious with yourself and others as we all walk through the process of seeking God in truth. When you question where someone may be in his or her journey toward holiness, refrain from judgment. Remain in prayer, good intention, and hopeful expectation for those seeking the path of righteousness, knowing that God sees our hearts and is well-pleased with those who seek to return to intimacy with Him, whatever that path may look like.

Food for Thought

- Do I believe that God is transforming me to live in a way that is best for myself and others around me?
- How will taking the guilt and shame away from this area of my life help me to live more freely and treat myself and others with more grace and kindness?
- How can I be more gracious with myself or others when the journey of transformation does not look the way I hope or expect?

Selah.

Living Your True Self

"Therefore, if anyone is in Christ, he is a new creation. The old has passed away; behold the new has come."

—2 Corinthians 5:7, ESV

The *false self* ego or persona we put on to create an image for ourselves and others to admire and praise leads to all kinds of anxieties and destruction. Truly, the false personas we create for ourselves may be the biggest idols we worship as humans. Caring so much about what others think of us and if we are reaching the often-impossible standards and goals we construct for ourselves leads to living inauthentic, unfulfilling lives. Yet worshiping our own egos and others is so rampant in our culture of self-seeking independence that it has become something to be admired and praised in a culture that has completely forgotten our divine purpose, making us beautiful and perfect in our own unique ways, without outside quantification to see if we measure up.

I Want to Break Free

When we forget God's purpose for creating us or we act as if we have nothing to do with it, we often miss the mark. Conversely, when we humbly acknowledge God's divine breath within us, we acknowledge

His power to transform us from mere humans to co-creators and coheirs in every good thing that the God of the universe has in store for a more abundant life.

When our souls aren't healthy, we can feel it in our lives—hardened, stressed, and lacking the joy we experienced before we started hiding under false ego. We keep the shell on for protection from the outside world, colliding in darkness with others who are just as heavily armored. It's no way to live, so engrossed in our own false selves that we end up hurting ourselves and others.

It's easy to see these hard shells on others but often more difficult to recognize the hardening of our own souls—that part of us that keeps us from opening up and being vulnerable after a lifetime of learned defensive response. Very real trauma can make this self-protection feel necessary, but the distance only serves to widen the gap between relationship with others, with God, and with our true selves.

When you consider that these connections are the very thing needed to heal the soul, it's no surprise to see that recovery groups like Alcoholics Anonymous and prison rehabilitation become breeding grounds for personal and spiritual discovery. It's when we reach such a humble state that our hard shells of false self fall away, and we're finally able to see our true worth and find joy in the openness and vulnerability that connects us to other people, to ourselves, and to God. Finally, we stop crashing hard shells against one another, as our relationships become a warm embrace of love.

Food for Thought

- What is the state of my soul? Have I become hardened and numb, or am I sensitive and alive to what God is putting in my heart and soul?
- Am I busy trying to prove myself? Or do I live in my true self, with nothing to prove or hide—vulnerable to share the best and worst of myself?

Selah.

Money Monster in My Soul

"But store up treasure for yourselves in heaven, where moths and vermin do not destroy, and where thieves do not break in and steal. For where your treasure is, there your heart will be also."

—Matthew 6:20–21

When we portray a false self-image, people who live from their souls can scare us. They're the kind of people who see past the hardened shell we've built around our hearts to protect us from the world. They look directly into who people are, which can be scary to those of us who hide our true selves under the cover of ego and false-self thinking.

Ring's Gone, Wall's Up

When I was 23, I went through something no *good Christian woman* ever expects: I got divorced. We went from happily ever after to struggling to feed his children before I knew it. Soon, we lost our home to the bank, and I spent years rebuilding my finances and cleaning up my credit. After the divorce, I hid completely in my false self (and if I am honest, I'm still trying to climb back out). From then on, I was determined to be an independent woman and never rely on anyone else again.

I built a wall around my heart to never again depend on someone who could possibly let me down—which detached me from all relationships, including myself, because no one could live up to my

29

perfect standards. I became the shrewdest businesswoman I could muster and worked hard to do more, become better, and be unfazed by anything or anyone who might get in my way. I was determined to become a billionaire so no one I loved would ever need to worry about finances again. I would take care of myself and my people—as if I were God Himself. And so I was blinded by my own pride and hard heart.

I still wanted a husband and family, but I was determined never to depend on an irresponsible person ever again. I still find it hard to allow others to take care of me in these same ways. My false self still feels the need to be in charge, always giving more than others, and I'm slowly learning to let it go. Though I still have goals and ambitions (and really, who wouldn't want to be a billionaire?), I'm learning to love myself and others in our imperfections, knowing that when we shoot for the moon and miss, we'll still land amongst the stars.

God's Got Me

With this simple shift in learning to let go of control and receive help, I have also begun to see the beauty of relying on God in every aspect of life. It's His grace that helps me rely on His other children, as well. My ego and false self tell me I'm God's only reliable child, that somehow He has appointed me as the protector and provider of the whole world. But my true self whispers that Jesus already did it all for me so I can rest in Him, placing all my hope in this truth. My true self reminds me that when I humble myself in the sight of the Lord, He will lift me up—that when I stop striving and just allow Him to use me, I will be able to do and become so much more for God, myself, and the world around me.

It's been a hard lesson to learn, but it's been invaluable. When we let our ego idols run rampant, we live in fear of the waves rolling in and washing away all the sand castle money temples we've built. But when we allow God to work out the way of provision, purpose, and love within the context of our true selves, we will become much less worried about losing these things, because we know that the things of God are eternal and cannot be lost.

Food for Thought

- Who do I know that lives mostly in their true self?
- In what ways do I try to carry the weight of the world as if I were God?
- In what ways can I rest in God, allowing myself to receive His blessings? How would this allow me to show up in the world in a more loving way?

Selah.

Nobody Likes a Fad Dieter

"Similarly, forcing your beliefs onto someone else damages
your relationship. The damage may not be easy to spot at
first, like tiny cracks in a wooden wheel, but it's just a matter
of time before the wheel splits apart."

—Derek Lin

You know that person who has lost forty pounds by going on some new fad diet and is now convinced that the entire world should do exactly what worked for them? Or the one who is on some new food craze every month? If you're like me, you probably try to avoid them. How much better is it when a person has had a significant lifestyle change so apparent that it causes people to ask questions? It's so much better to share your amazing health discoveries, tips, and encouragement when people say, "You're looking really healthy, what have you been doing?"

Not for Sale

The problem with trying to shove one's lifestyle choices down other people's throats is that nobody wants to be sold. For an idea to become our own, we reach our own conclusions. Man, I hated when my pastor would use this tactic with me. I would come to him with questions about life or spirituality, and he would never directly answer any of my questions. Instead, he would leave me with several more questions that

31

were actually pointing me down a path to the insights I was truly seeking. But I appreciated it so much more in the end.

The same goes for our spiritual lifestyles. Whether sharing your faith or interacting with others who express their spirituality in different ways, nobody wants to be sold a new belief system. My prayer is that we'll all live more like St. Francis of Assisi's famous quote: "Go out and preach the gospel, and when necessary, use words." I pray we would be so full of the fruits of the Spirit that people would see a significant difference in our lives.

When people see a difference in us, they tend to ask questions. They may ask how we can be peaceful in the midst of difficulties, loving in spite of injustice, or patient and faithful in ways that make no sense to them. When we live our lives in such a way, people will ask. And when they ask, they will find answers, as we open up about our faith and our God...now that their hearts want to hear.

When someone has lost a significant amount of weight or has a major physical health breakthrough and starts shouting their successes, tips, and newfound enlightenment from the rooftops, it's no surprise. At times, you might find it a little obnoxious, but their excitement is understandable. So, when you meet one of those Christians who wants to tell you all about how Jesus has transformed them from the inside out, consider their soul's metaphorical before and after photos, and try have some grace.

And extend that grace to yourself, as well. You're in a continuous process of transformation. Just as weight loss doesn't happen overnight, neither does spiritual health. Soul transformation takes ongoing spiritual nutrition and training.

Be the Change

So, how do we get to a place where people seek our perspective about the things of God? Developing the biblical fruits of the Spirit is a good start. Imagine what kind of world we would live in if everyone lived each day with love, joy, peace, patience, kindness, goodness, faithfulness, gentleness, and self-control.

When we invite people into our lives and truly care about theirs in love, it's amazing to see how they respond in kind. Joyful: Not unfazed by bad things in our lives, but choosing to trust in God's perfect plans despite things that make us sorrowful (which is where peace, patience, and faith also come into play). Gentle: With others as they express their thoughts, beliefs, and shortcomings; meeting them where they are in their journey and helping to light the path toward God's abundance. Self-controlled: Listening twice as much as we speak, so others feel loved, validated, and meaningful.

This kind of change in our lives makes people ask questions, makes them want the secret to happy living that you've got. It's not some fad diet we need to bandwagon. Our soul transformation changes us more and more into the image of God. People will take notice all on their own.

Food for Thought

- Does my spirituality manifest in a way that causes people to ponder or ask questions?
- How am I being daily transformed into the image of God I was created for?
- Do I feel the need to advertise my spirituality? If so, why?

Selah.

Bad PR

"The first step is admitting you have a problem."

—Rehab International

The only way we can bring positive change or forward movement to our lives is through awareness. How can we take steps to remedy situations that we are completely unaware of? We must look inward if we want to see change in our lives and in the world around us. If we want progress, we cannot keep living the same lives we were living yesterday. We must take a look at our lives and examine what we are doing that is producing the results we desire and the habits that result in outcomes we want to change.

Intentionally looking inward is the first step toward forward progress and positive change within ourselves and, ultimately, a similar change for the betterment of the world around us. If we desire to follow Mahatma Gandhi's advice to "be the change we wish to see in the world," we must examine what needs to change and recognize that it must first take place within us before it can be seen around us.

Trust Me, I Know

After the sting of my divorce, believing God was clearly unhappy with me, I decided to run from Him. As far and fast as I could, I ran into the cliché scene of sex, drugs, rock and roll, and all the things I had judged for so long. As much of the wrong way as this might have been, God truly does use *all* things together for our good, and not just the beautiful or put-together parts. During this time, I realized that not everyone who did drugs was a drug-dealing serial killer who was going to drug and rape me, as I had formerly believed. In fact, I actually had fun enjoying this crazy party lifestyle, for a while.

I was just like the story of the prodigal son living my life wildly. Though I didn't literally find myself eating pig slop, I was certainly consuming the soul-killing equivalent. I remember being curled up in my bed one evening crying out to God, "I still love You, I hope You still love me." I knew the way I was living was wrong, not just morally wrong in the sense of not being a rule-following *good girl,* but wrong in the sense that it was causing me to slowly die inside. I simply didn't see a way to change it in that moment. Though I wanted a life with God again, I kept living this way for a few years.

Over time, I slowly felt drawn back into God, but not quite like before. I decided I would try spirituality again. I no longer had a clue what that might look like, but I was determined to find a deeper truth, and I believed it was out there somewhere. After walking out of more churches than I could count—unable to handle what all seemed so fake, so contrived, and so money-grubbing—something still seemed to be missing. The same something that I had been missing in my former Christian life. I wanted to know Jesus again, but I knew there was more to it than I had previously known, and I wanted to discover what that was.

Eventually I reached out to my former pastor, who had stepped down from ministry after similar frustrations with the modern church. I asked if he knew of a church that I'd heard met in a bar, which I figured I could probably handle, since no image-obsessed Christian would be caught dead there.

I just wanted Jesus, not some glee club, concert, or community production to prop up my self-image as a good girl who does good things. I wanted to know God again, but I just wasn't finding Him at the mainstream churches I had tried attending. My former pastor suggested I visit an in-home small group that met on Sunday nights and just meditated for a while before discussing God. So, I got the details and agreed to check it out.

Driving up to the dark South Orange County suburb cul-de-sac, I found a free space under a streetlamp near the house and parked. Drawing my breath in, I let out a big *here goes nothing* sigh. There would be no easy escape route. No walking out of the audience here. At least that was one benefit to mega churches: total anonymity. You can get lost in the shuffle and leave. I didn't know anyone at this house except for the person who invited me, and I felt slightly awkward knocking on a stranger's door. Thankfully a kind lady walked up at the same time and introduced herself. As we walked in, she introduced me to others who were there for…what was it, *church?* Whatever it was, it was unlike any church or even small group I had ever been to before. Most people there were at least twice my age, and they all knew each other, yet somehow I was never an outsider from the moment I walked through the door.

There were no fake smiles handing me a pamphlet and sending me on my way, like I had experienced in other places, rather a strangely genuine look in the eyes of each person I met. I cautiously shared a little about myself and then chatted over a few healthy snacks with the people there. I felt strangely welcomed and at home.

We began some quiet meditation, which they called *contemplative prayer*, and I sat in silence, mostly wondering what this was all about. I had been a Christian before and spent time with so many Christians, but I didn't want anything to do with the kind of Christianity from my past. If there was another way to enter into what Jesus called life more

35

abundantly, I wanted to find out. If there was a different entry point, a more graceful, understanding, and truly loving way in, I wanted to know what it was.

The bell rang to indicate meditation was over, and the discussion began. I do not remember what the subject was, but I remember feeling comfortable enough to express my borderline heretical viewpoints on the issue. To my surprise, I was welcomed with expressions of curiosity and comments like, *Hmm, I never thought of it that way before.*

The anger in my questions abated a little when I discovered I would not be judged for differing opinions. It was odd, but delightful. This particular group of believers was not concerned with fitting me into their own theological boxes, but allowed me to find truth at my own pace and on my own journey with God that we were all on together. I was so fed up with the kind of Christianity that barked some boxed-up answer at me and told me exactly what I had to believe or I was out. I was so hurt by the kind of Christianity I had seen after my divorce when all my so-called Christian friends ditched me as if I were wearing a scarlet letter, but I cautiously proceeded to get to know this group of believers that seemed to simply accept me for me.

Telling people that their opinions are wrong never really helps them get closer to God, but acknowledging where they are and inviting them into greater truth is a much more effective and lasting path to closeness with the Creator. Moreover, I learned that I did not have to pretend to be more moral than I was or act like I was not sinful. It was assumed that we all were imperfectly perfect, and there was no need to hide it or discuss it unless it was somehow helpful. There was a freedom there that helped me to realize that God loved me anyway and so did these wonderful people. It was a rare environment to fall into, but I am blessed that my path to God led me to a place that made sense for me.

I know that not all Christian groups are as loving and accepting as this wonderful community. But I believe that, with prayer and discernment, everyone can find at least one person in the church who is sincerely loving, is honest without being judgmental, and listens and guides people on their own journey with Jesus.

36

Mystically Speaking

In my experience visiting various faith groups around the world, I've seen a small sector of the Christian community take this inward reflection for outward change by creating space for and giving priority to reflection and contemplation about God's will in their own lives, the Scriptures, and the world God loves. They begin an inward transformation that creates a ripple effect from their lives outward to the lives of those around them in their circle of influence.

This group of Christians is sometimes referred to as contemplatives or mystics. They engage in times of contemplative prayer, quiet sitting, or meditation, not just listening for answers but for a sense of closeness to their beloved Creator. In doing so, they seek to transform closer to the original perfection they were designed for. Not the rigid kind of perfection that many of us think of today, but the natural perfection we see in all God's creation. Like the beautiful symmetry reflected in a budding spring flower or dying autumn leaf.

These Christ-seekers have a completely different peace and an understanding about Christianity than those we see convincing people to *get saved* and buy their particular brand of Jesus. They live their faith in ways that others can't help but notice a profound difference. Something far more loving, peaceful, and gentle than one experiences within typical modern Christianity. They've become adept at listening for God's voice and finding His image in all of creation, so they tend to listen in a way that accepts and invites others to likewise share their own true selves.

These kinds of Christians radiate love—not because they're super human, but because they tend to move themselves out of the way to make room for Jesus to truly shine through them. In my experience, I have found contemplatives to truly display what it means to be *Christ-like*. And although they'd probably be the very last people to ever claim to have arrived at this end, the practice of contemplation is truly an aspect of seeking God that "transforms from glory to glory," as the Bible says.

What's God's Brand?

Many Christians throughout history have sadly done just the opposite. Religion has been used to control the masses rather than bring the freedom it was intended for, to wage war rather than the peace Jesus spoke of, to bring guilt and shame even though scripture clearly states there is no condemnation in Christ. Some well-meaning modern Christians preach their brand of Jesus as if He were a product to be sold—coming off like spiritual multi-level marketers, more concerned about how many people they can get in line for Jesus than actually seeing transformation in people's lives, much less their own.

It's easy to point the finger and act as if I am so much more spiritual than *those* kinds of Christians, but Richard Rohr reminds that we all start here on our journey to seeking truth. No judgment here, because I've surely been the worst offender and can easily slip back at a moment's notice.

The kind of Christian who tries to *recruit for Christ* without first having been personally transformed reminds me of a severely unhealthy person offering unsolicited diet advice to anyone who will listen. When we have truly been transformed, there is no need to shout from the rooftops about our transformation. There's no need to announce you've lost thirty pounds or increased your energy. When we have been transformed, people will notice.

I pray that this would be our spiritual aim. That people would know we follow Jesus by the way we love one another, listen to those around us, and care for the earth and all its inhabitants. Let's stop worrying about promoting Jesus and start living lives that promote Him for us.

How Do We Get There?

How do we get to that place where we are spiritually fit enough for people to notice? That the fruits of the Spirit are so evident in our lives that they inspire others to draw nearer to the God who created the universe? I believe a good first step is to **become present**, to begin to train our minds and spirits to stop rushing off into the future or lingering behind in the past. To train our spiritual muscles to return to God when we wander in thought, word, and action.

Although everyone's path to seeking God's truth is different, we know one thing for certain. Jesus promised in Matthew 7:7, "Seek and you will find." So keep seeking. The only thing we can do wrong when seeking God is give up…and even then, we can always begin again, always return, always seek, and always find.

The practice of taking down time can be a good way to enter into the present moment and become still and silent enough to hear God speaking to our spirit and changing our hearts to be more loving, kind, and peaceful. Much practice, prayer, and time are necessary for transformation to take place in our souls. Thankfully, we have more resources today than ever before to help guide us in seeking presence and truth through contemplative prayer and silent listening.[1]

Throughout scripture, God has called us to seek and find Him again and again. The Israelites constantly got it wrong in the Bible. Although He would leave them to their vices if they chose, He never quit pursuing them. Every time they cried out to Him, He would come to their rescue as if they had never betrayed Him. So, don't be afraid to cry out or let Him rescue you. Being transformed is never easy and what we find in our true selves may surprise us, but as we turn closer to His original design for our lives, I believe we will find again and again that it is so very good.

"'For I know the plans I have for you,' declares the Lord, "plans to prosper you and not to harm you, plans to give you hope and a future" (Jeremiah 29:11 NIV).

---

[1] Here are a couple of my favorite resources for developing contemplative practice:
- "Contemplative Prayer 'How To,'" YouTube video by The Soul Nutritionist Reina Rose, where I give a "how to" guide for developing the practice of contemplative prayer
- "Reflexion: A Spiritual Community," podcast and website, where I began my personal journey to recognizing God's Spirit in myself and others
- "The Soul Nutritionist Reina Rose" YouTube Channel also has several meditations and contemplative prayer videos for becoming present with God, self, and others.

Food for Thought

- Do I take time to sit quietly and listen to my soul and God's divine breath inside me?
- How can I become more present? How might that transform me from the inside out and affect my presence in the world?
- Do I believe that God is pursuing me? Could I believe it?

Selah.

Listening Practice

"I will instruct you and teach you in the way you should go; I will counsel you with my loving eye on you."

—Psalm 32:8, ESV

Following God often looks confusing and difficult. Sometimes, I've followed what I believed was God's voice in my heart in ways that didn't make any logical sense but eventually worked out for incredible blessings beyond all I could imagine or hope. Other times, I was so sure I heard from God, but things turned out nothing like expected. But the most frustrating are times when He's showed me things that involved the obedience of others who choose to go their own way. Never did I learn this more painfully than while living in South America in my late 20s, certain I was about to marry my Chilean fiancée, who broke off our engagement and sent my head spinning when he quickly married another woman instead shortly after (more on this later).

In times like these, timely sermons have reminded me that God doesn't force people to obey Him, and He sometimes moves on to others who will. As the prophet Samuel grieved King Saul's flawed leadership after his anointing to royalty, God told him to stop weeping and go anoint David, who would go on to be the nation's greatest leader. Samuel didn't hear God wrong when he first anointed Saul, but when the flawed king freely chose to go his own way, God called Samuel to quit mourning over Saul's disobedience and move on to

David. Through His biblical stories, God reminds me to trust in the ways that He speaks to me, holding His promises loosely in my hands, knowing that He will work all things together for good.

Results Show When You Put in the Time

If we want to be healthy, we need to follow a healthy lifestyle of food and exercise. Statistics show that spending the bulk of our time with people who have healthy habits will increase our chances of staying in shape and feeling great. If we eat fast food every day, we surely won't look or feel the way we desire. The same is true for our souls. If we desire to experience more abundant life from Jesus, we must spend time with Him, do as He does, and incline our hearts to living the life He embodied and taught.

Sometimes it takes a while for us to see God's blessings play out. Like in the Bible's story about Ruth, a foreign widow who arrived in Israel with no hope, money, or real prospects but worked hard and eventually remarried into abundance, eventually developing Jesus' lineage. Or Joseph, whose brothers despised his God-given visions and sold him into slavery, where he worked for decades before eventually seeing his leadership premonitions come to fruition. Though his dreams were eventually realized, many trials taught Joseph to exercise discernment in sharing his gift. Had he given up through any of the personal injustices he experienced along the way, Joseph may never have ended up in the right place at the right time to save himself, his family, and the entire region from starvation in the coming famine.

It goes so much further than the *what would Jesus do* cliché. When you begin to trust and follow Christ, you will start to ask the right questions, seek the right things, and knock on the right doors. To continue seeking to be more like Him, we must spend time with Him, and there are so many ways to do that.

Not just with a quick prayer here and there, but in constant conversation like with a best friend. Talk to Jesus throughout your day—throw Bluetooth headphones in your ear if you start to get funny looks. Then when you feel yourself heading too far in the wrong direction, take time to develop awareness and turn yourself around.

Course-Correct and Move On

So many times, Jesus asks people to follow Him by living out His teachings full of love, joy, peace, patience, kindness, goodness, faithfulness, and self-control. Yet too often, we slowly allow sin into our lives until it becomes an addiction, large or small. Eventually, our aim begins to slowly move off the mark, until it's off the target entirely. The particular sins and their size don't matter, the important thing is to become aware enough to recognize when we are missing the mark and correct our aim.

Christians call this *confessing and repenting of our sins*—simply to stop and correct our aim—essentially saying sorry; I want to do better. *Confess* and *repent* are pretty triggering words in the Christian faith. (And for others, they can sound just downright off-putting.) These words can inspire guilt and shame, but there's really no need. After all, how can you correct something you won't even admit to yourself or to God? As Alcoholics Anonymous notes: "The first step is admitting we have a problem." That's confession—owning up to our own flaws— and repentance is simply turning around and walking the other direction.

If sinning is missing the mark, consider: Are you mindlessly flinging emotional, relationship, and goal-related arrows into an abyss of apathy and despair? Or do you feel content, like your life is hitting the target, maybe even the bull's-eye?

Sit with this thought and listen to where God may be leading you. Maybe He will give you hints on how to improve your aim, maybe He'll show you a new target, maybe He will sit with you and increase your presence and awareness of His nearness to you. Or perhaps you will experience nothing. Whatever your expectations or hang-ups, try giving them to God and trusting our good Father to give you the hope and future that He promises.

Food for Thought

- Who do I give most of my time? (Is God anywhere toward the top of the list?)
- What are some ways God speaks to my heart? Do I take time in silence to try to listen to Him?
- Is there an area of life I need to repent or change directions?

Selah.

Biblical Wisdom

"Because of the increase of wickedness, the love of most will grow cold."

—Matthew 24:12 NIV

Pope Francis quoted this verse in his 2018 Lent message of holiness. The practices of biblical wisdom and seeking God through prayer seems to have eluded our current culture so much that it is difficult to imagine a way back. "The love of many growing cold" feels pretty dead-on in today's society. How many people are afraid to express their love to one another? Or afraid of being rejected by the cold hearts of others? How many have taught themselves to be cold and unfeeling in order to fit into a culture that considers it a badge of honor to engage in relationships without getting attached or involved?

Does it have to be this way? Is it too late to re-learn how to love again?

Melt Our Cold Hearts, Oh God

Once again, the Bible has the answer to society's problems, if we take the time and effort to follow its teachings. Jesus talks a lot about grace and love. In fact, he calls loving others the greatest commandment. There's a reason: Grace and love go hand in hand. And as we learn how to accept God's grace and love for us, we'll start to do the same for others. The wonderful thing about God's grace is that He offers it again and again, as we prayerfully begin to fail upward. Hopefully failing a little closer to the mark each time.

The idea of reshaping our cultural identity makes me think of babies learning to walk. Unfortunately, we won't all start walking around more loving and Christ-like the minute we start following Jesus. But infants don't simply get up and start walking around either. It's a process that takes time and some stumbles along the way. Like parents encouraging their children every time they fall, God expects the falls, calling our names and beckoning us to keep going. If we can simply accept it, reach out and take hold of it, this grace and love is ours for the sharing.

In the world at large, biblical wisdom isn't valued much these days. But how can the teachings of love, grace, and learning through our failures ever become irrelevant? These lessons may not be appreciated in a culture of success at all costs and getting to the top regardless of whether it costs us everything that truly matters, yet it is a message that is desperately needed in a culture that I believe is waking up to the errors of its ways. A culture that is opening its eyes to the lies that materialism and hedonism have pledged and left unpaid.

What is even more disheartening is how coldly we see Christians interacting in today's society. So much of mainstream Christian culture has drifted so far from gospel grace and freedom, right back into the moralistic scorekeeper mentality that Jesus warned against. It's so easy to get caught up in trying to win some sort of Christian game by simply keeping all the rules. I confess that I often tend to lean toward the moralistic and judgmental forms of thinking because it seems so much more structured and safe than actually loving and living in graceful non-judgment of self and others.

Literally Missing the Point

In this age of technology and increased learning, we've started to societally pat ourselves on the back for being so enlightened, yet the reverse has actually happened. Feelings can't be viewed under a microscope or quantified on a spreadsheet, and so we've started to live our faith in blacks and whites, ignoring anything in the grey. We've put Christianity into a box.

The Bible's wisdom is taught through a mix of literal and figurative stories, poems, and songs. But many religious people today have forgotten how to experience a poem, feel a message, or accept something as truth without first interpreting it completely literally. This extreme literalism is relatively new in Christianity's millennia-long history, but it has asserted its authority over the religious world and wreaked havoc and hatred within it. Since the 16th-century Reformation's religious leaders sought to match the Rationalistic philosophy of the time, Western Christianity in particular has suffered these effects. Instead of abiding by what Paul called "knowing spiritual things in a spiritual way," religion has sought to know spiritual things in a concrete and rational way that just does not align with the entire concept of spirituality.

Yet, perhaps we can wake up and see that the moment we think we know everything is often precisely when we find that we know nothing, that pride comes before a fall and the humble are lifted up. Perhaps as a culture, we will learn to humble ourselves and ask questions again, to seek and find, to knock and have the door answered, and to learn to live in the enchantment of the mystery. Maybe then, we'll learn how to truly love again.

Food for Thought

- Have I let the love in my heart grow cold because it seems safe?
- What are my thoughts on biblical wisdom? How does it apply to my life, if at all?
- Do I like to have certain, concrete answers to spiritual questions, or do I accept that things may always remain a mystery?

Selah.

PART 2:
Set up Your Soul for Success

Our influence over others is powerful. There is a reason our parents warn us about peer pressure and get concerned when we are developing what they consider the *wrong type of friends*. Our personal relationships have more influence over our lives than just about any other factor. We set ourselves up for success by selecting and spending more time with those who build us up, encourage us, and allow us to do likewise in their lives as well. So, it's no surprise that the company we keep impacts our soul.

Five Wise Friends

"Whoever walks with the wise becomes wise, but the
companion of fools will suffer harm."

—Proverbs 13:20

Have you ever tried to start a fitness routine on your own, only to find yourself sleeping in three days after you committed to waking up early to jog? Staying motivated on our own can be difficult; good friends who inspire and encourage can make all the difference between talking about having a great life and actually having a great life.

Motivational speaker Jim Rohn famously teaches that we become the collective average of the five people we spend the most time with. Harvard Medical School research shows our social networks greatly influence the direction and quality of our lives in every aspect, from our weight to the amount of money we make. Is it any wonder that the book of Proverbs points out time and again that we become like the people we're around?

Evaluating the Company We Keep

It cannot be stressed enough how important it is to choose the people we spend large quantities of time with very wisely. A good start might be to seek out people you desire to become like and make an effort to spend time with them. This does not mean to ditch all your friends for better ones, but if you look around and realize that becoming like anyone you are currently spending time with makes you cringe even a little, it might be time for a change.

I will be the first to admit that even as a former fitness instructor, I am quite prone to the peer pressure of eating sugary and fatty foods when in the company of friends and family who like to indulge. I notice that if I am not intentionally watching what I eat or avoiding certain foods, I will almost always gain at least five pounds every time I visit home for a few weeks. I actually don't mind the extra curves, but my body doesn't seem to operate on all cylinders when I am not giving it good fuel.

In her NewYork.com article about obesity and social interaction, writer Gina Kolata suggests I'm not alone in my propensity to put on the pounds when spending time with certain loved ones. She writes: "Obesity can spread from person to person, much like a virus, according to researchers. When one person gains weight, close friends tend to gain weight, too."

Obesity's like a virus that spreads from person to person?! That is a pretty bold statement. However, research shows that our body mass index isn't all that's affected by the company we keep—but every aspect of life.

Soul Nourishment

Having been blessed to travel the world for a living has also meant I've spent a lot of time on the go, so my presence in town is always considered a special occasion. My friends go out of their way to spend time with me, so perhaps they have that extra drink or dessert that they would have forgone if we weren't considering our time together to be such a rare treat. I'm so grateful for each and every one of my cherished friends around the world, who make me feel so special. It feels like a special treat for me to see them too, and before I realize it,

I've often indulged in some less-than-body-friendly foods and drinks, while living to enjoy each moment spent with the people I love. But now that I'm aware, I can be more mindful.

More important than the food that nourishes our bodies is the nourishment we provide our souls and those around us. Over the years, I have carefully selected the people I spend the most time with, who will nourish my soul. It may be a few more than five, but Rohn's theory still stands. I choose to surround myself with people who will put the same love and care into our relationship that I want in my life—setting aside time to connect in person, to call and check in even though I'm not much of a "phone person," to believe in me, and to support my seemingly impossible goals and plans. They think I am crazy in the best possible way. They're my cheerleaders, as I am theirs, and we're all better for it.

Food for Thought

- Who are the five people I spend the most time with? Do I want to be like these people?
- Who influences me the most? If I become like the people I spend the most time with, have I chosen wisely?
- What influence do I have on others?

Selah.

Recognizing Unhealthy Influences

"Therefore, encourage one another and build each
other up…"

—1 Thessalonians 5:11, NIV

When you start to examine the company you keep in the context of who you want to be, you will likely come to realize a hard truth: Some relationships are no good for your soul. As I've developed wisdom and started learning what nourishes my own soul, I've learned to identify and distance myself from toxic people in my life, sometimes within my own Christian circles. It took time and discernment, listening to God with courage to be my true self, to determine my worthwhile friendships. But through the good and bad experiences that got me here, I now look around and see a wonderful group of international friends who all make meaningful contributions to my life.

Friend or Faux?

After my brother died, I moved to the Midwest to start a new life. Driving past his work, apartment, and favorite spots left me in tears, and I simply had to get out. So I followed a long-distance relationship with the promise of a fresh start in the great unknown and got my first taste of the deceptive ease of running from my problems, rather than confronting them. It didn't go well.

Nothing sets the rumor mill running like a California "hippie" in the middle of America. It wasn't long after I'd gotten involved with the young adults at a local church—developing what I thought was a pretty good group of friends—that the chatter started to make its way back to me.

In the two weeks before my new apartment was ready, my boyfriend had graciously offered to let me stay with him, and now speculation about our purity set this religious community ablaze. *We were living together in sin.* When the words reached my ears, my blood boiled. It didn't matter that he'd previously asked to marry me, that he'd politely taken the couch, or even that he was still a virgin. Because that's the thing about rumors: There's no room for truth.

I never understood why some people hated Christians until this moment. But when a friend shared the gossip, all I could think was, *If they really believed this, shouldn't these so-called Christians follow their teachings and love me through this rather than talk behind my back?!* Red flag number one.

As I started to settle in and get to know people better, I began sharing some of my goals and dreams. Before long, the gossip mill started turning again, and I learned they were mocking me behind my back. Red flag number two.

I was just about done with these so-called Christians, when they started teaching some very fundamental-literalistic points of view, saying *everything* in the Bible is meant exactly literally. Weren't these the

50

same people who had ignored the Bible's teachings on gossip? I got up and walked out of the church thinking, *Then you all would have lost your hands and eyes because surely everyone has stolen or lusted at some point in life!* Three red flags, and these people were out in my mind.

Usually, my ego would have tried to win over the haters and make everyone like me, but time with God taught me I didn't need these people in my circle of influence. I still keep in touch with a select few from that time in my life, those who spoke and thought differently, seeking God's truth in their lives. Selecting these people and letting the others take their gossip and go on their merry way has made my life and relationships better today. And I learned a valuable lesson that claiming you're a Christian does not mean you're automatically living a life that nourishes the soul.

None of My Business

Some people just won't like you. It's a harsh reality, but it doesn't have to break your heart. In fact, most of the time, I have found that someone's bias against me really had nothing to do with me and everything to do with their own insecurities. The sooner you learn this, the happier you will be.

The first time I became aware of this was a sunny summer afternoon just days before my best friend's wedding. Her family had become like an extended family to me, and I felt so special to be a part of this occasion, as the only non-related bridesmaid in the ceremony. Alone at the house with my friend's generally grumpier older sister, I busied myself with preparations until she scooted closer and looked me in the eye. "I'm sorry for being so mean to you all these years," she shocked me to my core. "I've always been so rude to you because you've been more of a sister to my sister than I have been. I'm sorry. Will you please forgive me?"

My mind reeled with this new information. I was flabbergasted. *You didn't like me? I just thought you were a grumpy person.* I mulled this over in my mind for a moment before collecting myself enough to say, "Um, of course I forgive you."

In the years since, I've met more people who haven't liked me for one reason or another. Some were annoyed with my bubbly personality. Others simply disliked my closeness with others in their lives. But short of being an actively bad friend to my best friend, there was nothing I could have done to make her sister like me. I just had to be myself and hope for the best.

Sometimes I miss my naiveté about other people's opinions of me. I see a sour expression or catch something from the gossip mill, and my people-pleasing inner child goes into overdrive. One dear friend even once told me she used to want to break my guitar over my head because I seemed too happy all the time. But if my joyous kindness is annoying to someone, then that's their problem, not mine.

If we go through life letting other people's negative opinions of us change our opinion of ourselves, we'll never have a firm foundational sense of self. But if we keep ourselves focused on what we are called to do and decide that other people's negative opinions of us are none of our business, we will live much happier and more encouraged to become all we were created to be.

In the same way, let's commit to building people up in life and expressing the good we see in them. It may seem weird at first, but once that initial feeling subsides, you will see your relationships and the people around you blossom under the showers of your praise and encouragement.

"How would your life be different if you walked away from gossip and verbal defamation? Let today be the day you speak only the good you know of other people and encourage others to do the same."

—Steve Maraboli,
Life, the Truth, and Being Free

Food for Thought

- In what ways do I let other people's opinions of me affect my thoughts and feelings about myself?
- What proactive steps can I take to refrain from saying negative things about myself and others?
- Am I secure enough in who I am to not be affected by others opinions of me?
- How can I ask God to help me become more secure in who I am?

Selah.

Texas-Sized Faith

"So if you sinful people know how to give good gifts to your
children, how much more will your heavenly Father give
good gifts to those who ask Him!"

—Matthew 7:11 NLT

As I stood outside the tiny World War II-era home of a girl I had never met, I retraced my thoughts to how exactly I'd gotten there. *It probably wouldn't be faith if it didn't sound crazy*, my pastor had answered when I told him it sounded crazy. But here I was, clenching all my worldly possessions in two bags, standing on the doorstep at the home of a girl I knew nothing about in a city I'd never been before. There was no turning back now. I'd followed what felt like God's direction for my life, and He was definitely in control now.

How Had I Gotten Here?

Like most stories of faith, it started in despair. Nursing a broken heart after my broken engagement in South America, I'd moved back to my hometown in Southern California, where I'd started attending as many churches as I could find several times a day. Christian, Catholic, English-speaking, Spanish—I went to them all. I was in so much need of Christ's love that I would go anywhere and do anything to be closer to Him in those moments.

I remember my pastor telling me to cherish those moments in my heart, because there is a closeness in the depths that we often do not know in the heights. I did not understand it at the time, but I know it now. These "dark nights of the soul" draw me to my knees and cause me to fall on my face before God in prayer, creating an intimacy with Him that cannot seem to be matched in the times of joy and gladness. There is a different intimacy in those times, but the way He draws near and comforts during the dark times is something more heartwarming than words could fully describe.

During this time of church and prayer and more church, I started praying, talking, and thinking about going to Houston. One week, just about every Bible study I watched or attended spoke about taking action, which was the push I needed. So, I bought my one-way ticket and moved to Texas.

Faith in Action

It was far from easy, but God parted Red Seas for me everywhere I went. And so I stood at the door, knocking. I had researched my couch-surfing host as well as I could: plenty of good reviews, dating back several years, with nothing bad that I could find. That should serve as sufficient evidence that she wasn't going to cut me up into bits and hide me in her basement refrigerator. "Here goes nothing," I whispered under my breath and walked up the front porch steps to meet a girl who would soon become one of my best friends and most faithful prayer partners.

As I opened up and shared the hurts and hopes that brought me to her home, she started sharing her own praises and pains. We became fast friends. Support system? Check. Things were starting to fall into place. I had two job offers my first week in Texas, and another friend in town lent me her swanky convertible long-term while I got on my feet. Check and check. Now I just needed a permanent address, which proved easier said than done.

My faithful prayer warrior friend let me stay with her for a month to look for my own place to live without the pressure of a time crunch, and my hunt was on. I remember coming back to her house after a particularly difficult day. As I unlocked the door to her beautiful home in an idyllic neighborhood, I reflected on the tiny room I'd just visited far on the outskirts of town, covered in filth. I remember throwing myself on the bed in pity and wept giant Disney Princess-style tears—thinking *I moved to a dump! How could I have done this with my life?*—before sobbing myself to sleep.

During that month, my Prayer Warrior Princess friend and I connected on a deep level, sharing our joys and pains together, as we began a sort of ritual of soul improvement, exercise, and communion together nearly every day. I remember crying together about the state of our lives in those moments: her on depression medications, contemplating dropping out of her doctorate program, and fearing losing her best friend with whom she was secretly in love and me slowly recovering from the disillusionment of a failed South American engagement.

But our faithfulness to God and our new friendship soon saw fruit, as my Prayer Warrior Princess helped me find a home of my own in her idyllic community and time settled our various difficulties and pains.

Praise be to God, about a year-and-a-half later, we laughed at ourselves as we took communion together, crying tears of joy about how our lives had changed. She had finished the doctorate she considered abandoning, was a professor at the university of her dreams, and had just married the very person she was so afraid of losing just a year prior. I was traveling around the world and getting paid to do so, singing for a church in Monaco, and finally realized my dream of sponsoring orphans and traveling to Russia to visit them.

She thanked me for introducing communion to her in a new way. She said she had always come to it with a sense of unworthiness, but the way we took communion together helped her to come to God with the confidence of one of His loved children, instead of as a groveling worm. While it's true that we will never be good enough to earn God's love or salvation, we must always remember that He formed us from the closest of relationships that our minds can comprehend because of how deeply and passionately He loves us.

Spending all this time together with the Lord brought my Prayer Warrior Princess and I so close together. We came to God with all our hurts, all of our brokenness, and He repaired us. And now that perfect stranger, whose doorstep my faith in God's goodness led me to, has become my first call every time I need prayer in my life.

He is a good Father who gives good gifts to His children, better than any earthly parent could ever hope to give. It doesn't always look like we expected, but it's always exceedingly, abundantly more than we could have hoped or imagined, as we simply let go of trying to control it all and put our trust in God and His plans.

Food for Thought

- What does it look like to let go of control and put trust in God's plans?
- What is the difference between foolishness and trusting in God?
- In what areas of life would I benefit from trusting and having more faith in God's good plans for me?
- Do I believe God is good and has my back? How can I pray for Him to reveal this to me more clearly?

Selah.

Mind Sparring

"Like iron sharpens iron, so one person sharpens another."

—Proverbs 27:17

I love to do something I call *mind sparring* with close friends who share different values and goals. We brainstorm ideas and toss concepts back and forth until we both get a better perspective or at least enjoy an in-depth conversation learning something that can be applied to becoming better, more focused, or more motivated in some way. Doing this reminds me of my brother.

He was an eclectic guy: a big, motorcycle-riding, MMA-training, computer-fixing hairdresser. One day, we'd be coloring my hair together, the next we'd be training together at his local martial arts gym, where he would spar with other guys practicing for everything from exercise for fun to training for an upcoming fight.

The purpose of sparring is to practice with better people so that you can improve your skills in a safer environment, rather than in an actual fight. But even in practice, injuries can happen. Even when you don't mean to, you can cause pain. This was the case when my big bear of a brother came home one day after a sparring session, feeling horrible for accidentally breaking a sparring partner's collarbone. He never meant to, but my brother still felt bad for hurting the guy. Similarly, giving advice can easily turn into mental sparring, especially in a mentor relationship, and feelings can accidentally get hurt without intention.

I have a dear friend whom I've been mentoring for a long time who came to me for advice about a difficulty with her new boyfriend. When she told me her story, I could not see anything he had done wrong. In fact, all I could see was his attempt to show her love, as she got upset. I had known them both since they were kids, and I told her my sincere opinion. I told her that I believed she was in the wrong, that he was just trying to be good to her, and she was acting prideful and childish in her response.

She didn't appreciate this assessment in the moment and went away feeling hurt. I left the evening feeling as bad as my brother did when he broke that guy's collarbone. However, the next day she called and, to my surprise, she thanked me. She realized she had been being mean to her boyfriend, perhaps only to protect her own heart from liking him too much. She thanked me for not being a shallow friend who would just agree with everything she said and encourage her to break up with him, as some of her peers at the time would do. We agreed that it takes a real friendship to tell someone the truth, especially when we are in the wrong. This pair is still together today and happily married. Thank God for the advice of true friends and for loving understanding between couples.

"Truth without love is brutality, and love without truth
is hypocrisy."

—Warren W. Wiersbe, writer

Food for Thought

- Which of my friends sharpens my mind and spirit? Who do I have my most meaningful conversations with?
- What kinds of conversations enliven my soul?
- Which topics make me most passionate?

Selah.

Modern Mentorship

"Without counsel, purposes are disappointed; but in the multitude of counselors, they are established."

—Proverbs 15:22, KJV

The biblical advice for living a wise life includes having a multitude of wise counselors. If only wise counselors grew on trees! But what if wise counselors are hard to come by in your current environment? What if you don't even know what to look for when it comes to wise counsel? Is there any hope for such a situation? Luckily, we live in a time when people can have many types of mentors in many different ways.

When we notice that the people we give our time have an influence on us, it also brings awareness to the influence we have on others. We can be the change we wish to see in the world, spreading love and kindness from one person to the next. We can also start to pay attention to whether we are being more influenced by others instead. And if we don't like that influence, we can make efforts to bring more beneficial relationships into our lives.

Wise Counsel

Maybe you don't have a group of friends who are moving in the direction you would like to head. Don't worry; it is possible to find a mentor within the pages of a book written by a wise author, watch a sermon by a pastor who resonates with you, or spend time alone with God learning to become still enough to "hear" Him to speaking to your heart.

The Bible has so much to say about wisdom. It says wisdom is more precious than silver, gold, or any other riches we could hold in our hands. Wisdom cannot be taken away. It also says that wisdom is found in a variety of wise counselors. Seek mentors who will ask the right questions to lead you toward the answers you seek.

Mentorship in Unlikely Places

Nobody is an expert in a day. In areas of health, spirituality, business, finances, or relationships, we will fail—it is simply a part of life. If we commit to improvement, seek wisdom through personal reflection, books, tools, and wise counselors; however, we can quit repeating the past and start living a better future.

The wonderful thing about living in the information age is that there are many ways we can "spend time" with the people who we want to influence our lives. Books, tools, and videos can turn virtual strangers into some of our greatest mentors.

Even if the people around you are not the mentor material you are seeking, we live in an age where you can find wise and godly counsel beyond your immediate circle, beyond your region, and beyond the current level of wisdom or faith in your social sphere.

When I was starting my first businesses, I watched business and investment advice speeches from Bill Gates and Warren Buffett. I didn't know anyone at the time who owned their own business, and I made a lot of mistakes that would have been a lot easier to navigate with a mentor. But I didn't have any in-person mentors at the time, so I read, listened to, and watched all the material I could get my hands on to at least start stumbling upward.

Though I now meet with many mentors on a regular basis throughout the world, I also consider quite a few people to be my cyber mentors. When I am not in one of my hometowns, where I can sit with a cup of coffee and glean wise advice from my favorite mentors in person, I can listen to some of my favorite Bible teachers online and hear what they have to say on a multitude of subjects. Hearing wise counsel through sermons on many different topics, I have access to great biblical minds of our day, many of whom have fed into my spiritual life at one point or another, with the precise message I needed at the moment I needed it most.

The Ultimate Mentor

Regardless of whether you find your mentors in person or elsewhere, remember that the ultimate mentor is "18 inches from the floor," as Baptist pastor Charles Stanley likes to put it. On our knees before God, we can be sure that He will be faithful to meet us and guide us—even if that guidance is to sit and wait in His presence for an answer that is still a long time coming.

There's no need to try to pray perfectly or say all the right things, you can just talk to God and listen for answers. He is always faithful to hear the prayers of His people.

When we prayerfully commit to becoming conscious of our lives and our intentions, we can become a wise friend to someone else. By seeking out mentors both in person and through the tools available to us, we can then pass that wisdom on to those who come after us. I'm so grateful for the many mentors in my own life, and I am also grateful for those who have blessed me by allowing me to become a mentor to them.

I encourage you to pray about the people and things you allow into your own soul. Remember to weigh everything with prayer and God's teachings to check the counsel for yourself. If a subject troubles you, ask God if that's because He is challenging your heart to change something difficult in your life or if it's because you are hearing misguided information. Read what God's Word has said on the subject and continue to lift it up in prayer and silent listening as you wait on God to give you peace one way or another.

Food for Thought

- Are my closest relationships people that I am happy to have influencing me?
- Do I have wise counselors in my life? Who are they? Are they people I want to be like?
- Am I a good example to the people around me?

Selah.

Group Fitness

"Do not give up meeting together, as some are in the habit of doing, but encouraging one another—and all the more as you see the Day approaching."

—Hebrews 10:25, NIV

In the book of Romans, Paul says that faith comes by hearing God's Word. It just so happens this is also a great way to consume our spiritual nutrition. Audio Bibles and apps, preacher podcasts and YouTube videos, and church websites have never been easier to access than now. Regardless of the means, a steady diet of God's Word is like a big bowl of zucchini pasta for the soul: It'll leave you filled with daily spiritual nutrition, rather than spiritually famished or void of nutrition.

It's so easy to listen to scripture during a daily commute, a workout, or even while doing simple tasks like cleaning the house, but I find it even more fulfilling when I have plenty of free time and can sit in front of my computer, with my journal in hand to take notes on what I'm listening to. It is like sitting down to slowly savor a gourmet meal as opposed to scarfing down a veggie wrap on the way to a meeting.

Created for Community

Listening to preaching, however, is not a great substitute for attending church altogether. I discover this every year when I am in certain parts of the world where I have little to no community. Despite still reading my Bible, praying, and hearing others' teachings, our souls still crave being in relationship with others.

God created us to share this life with other people. We see it from the very beginning of the creation story to the end of the Bible. In the creation story, everything was all so good—until the first thing God said was not good, for man to be alone.

Food for Thought

- What resources can I access if I want to learn more about the Bible and its teachings?
- When is a good time in my day to start listening to soul-nourishing information?
- How do I feel about attending a faith-based community? How might this nourish my soul?

Selah.

Change Your Environment, Change Your Life

"When it comes to relationships, we are greatly influenced—whether we like it or not—by those closest to us. It affects our way of thinking, our self-esteem, and our decisions. Of course, everyone is their own person, but research has shown that we're more affected by our environment than we think."

—Aimee Groth, You're The Average Of The Five People You Spend The Most Time With, BusinessInsider.com

Our environment affects how we think, how we act, and what we do. If we are at the gym, we are likely working out; if we are in the dance studio, we're most likely dancing. Likewise, it would not be appropriate to be working out or dancing in a classroom full of people preparing to take an exam, nor would it make sense to sit down and take an algebra exam on a crowded dance floor. Our environment influences who we meet and spend time with.

It makes me think of a community I joined that is made up of people from all parts of the globe seeking to expand themselves, learn more, and create a better impact on the world around them. There was an event coming up, and I thought to myself, *This is the kind of environment I need to place myself in if I want to surround myself with people who will inspire me to grow and expand.* The environments we are in effect the people we spend time with, and the people we spend time with influence our lives perhaps more than any other factor.

The Power of No

Some environments are easier to change than others. If you live in a bad neighborhood, it's not necessarily easy to just pick up and move away from bad influences. But we can be more aware of the environments that influence our behaviors that are ultimately harmful to our souls. Just as a bar is a dangerous place for an alcoholic, bringing awareness to the less obvious temptations in our lives can help change any behaviors we don't want.

Window shopping might not be the best pastime for a shopaholic trying to get out of debt, and hanging out in a smokers' corner probably isn't the best spot for someone trying to quit. In their book Will Power, authors John Tierney and Roy Baumeister suggest that every person has a finite amount of willpower. Once used up for the day, a person becomes more susceptible to making poor choices than they would have done before their willpower was depleted. When we are full of energy, well fed, and not already exhausted by a multitude of choices throughout the day, we tend to make better choices. But the authors also note that those who give themselves fewer opportunities to need to use it maintain the highest amounts of willpower.

Avoiding Temptations

High-level performers seem to have this concept down to a science and exploit its benefits by shaping their morning routines to ease the potential for making bad choices. Some executives wear the same basic outfit each day to eliminate the need for unnecessary decision-making that would deplete their precious stores of willpower.

Like Facebook creator Mark Zuckerberg, who has said he wears multiple versions of the same grey T-shirt every day to clear his life of unnecessary choices so he can "make as few decisions as possible about anything except how to best serve the community." The value of conserving willpower for making important decisions is a good example to examine what daily actions steal our own willpower from making more important decisions in our own lives. While I'm not yet ready to start wearing the same dress every day, I have definitely begun to examine which decisions are more important in my life and avoid leaving them to the end of the day when I'm tired, hungry, and less likely to make good choices.

The Bible says that people with the most willpower flee from temptation. They don't keep the candy in the house, they refrain from visiting their significant others late at night if they've decided not to have sex, and they take alternative routes to avoid passing by an irresistible sale when they know they need to reign in the spending. They do this by controlling their environment.

Consciously choosing a healthy environment ahead of time gives a home court advantage that puts us in a place to make better decisions and decreases the likelihood of succumbing to temptations that rarely, if ever, fulfill. Which environments tempt you to do things that make your soul feel empty once the high of the experience has come and gone? What better environments could you spend your time in instead, or other activities you could participate in? Could you make environmental changes ahead of time for the good of your soul?

Food for Thought

- Which habits or environments positively affect my life?
- Which habits or environments cause me to make poor choices?
- How can I be more intentional about the environments and habits I choose?

Selah.

Heaven on Earth

"The kingdom of God has come upon you."

—Luke 11:20, NIV

What better environment could we ever imagine than heaven? Not the white fluffy clouds, wings, and harps after death that we've been conditioned to imagine, but the biblical description of heaven here on earth if we are willing and aware enough to tap into it. This is the heaven that embodies love, joy, peace, patience, kindness, goodness, faithfulness, gentleness, and self-control—as much here and now as it is after this physical life is over.

Unfortunately, heaven on earth does not mean living in a state of eternal bliss, never experiencing any pain or distress. Living heaven on earth is about a change of heart that enables us to rise up during times of pain and distress, rather than being crushed underneath them. It's like seeing earth and its problems through grateful, heaven-colored glasses—being able to see people and their issues through the lens of God's love, His image in them, in ourselves, and in the world around us. When we draw near to the God who brings beauty from ashes and life from death, we begin to see this beauty all around us.

Change of Heart

Many of us have come to think of salvation and the kingdom of God as some sort of eternal fire insurance policy for after we die. But when Jesus instructs His followers to pray, He specifically says, "Your kingdom come, Your will be done on earth as it is in heaven" (Matthew 6:10). His kingdom is available for us in this lifetime, as well as in the next. He teaches us to desire God's will here on earth and to seek His kingdom now.

Jesus' teaching is an invitation into a better way to live now. He said that all who hear the Word of God and keep it will be blessed. Simple. Not necessarily easy, but simple.

The Gospel Transformation Bible's commentary on Luke 11 explains hearing and keeping the Word of God, noting "the gospel is not a call to perform in order to get God's favor; rather, it is a call first to hear—to receive the message of God's kindness and love—and then to be transformed by the Spirit's work. From this basis, and constantly buoyed by grace, we strive to follow after Jesus."

I love this commentary because it is so different from the traditional notion that the Pharisees of Jesus' time believed: If we do the right things perfectly, then we will be blessed. Or a modern rendition: If you're a good person, then you will be rewarded with a free pass to heaven after you die. Doing the right things is certainly part of the equation, but *why* are we doing the right things?

I can attest from both personal experience and observation that those who strive to do the right things rarely do. Consider people who are severely out of shape—especially those who, sadly, attach emotions of guilt and condemnation to food choices. They may very likely be able to resist the foods their bodies have been biochemically addicted to for years, only to find themselves at the bottom of a box of Oreos before the week is out. Trying to change our behaviors isn't what brings about change; developing strong convictions for why we want to change them is crucial.

What's Your Why?

Any success-related seminar worth its weight will likely focus less on what to do and more on why things are done. In many motivational conferences, participants are told to develop a strong *why* for what they are doing. The idea is that, when you remind yourself of the *why*, you can bear whatever it takes to get to your intention or goal.

If that person simply focuses on not eating an entire box of Oreos (the *what*) without a strong reason not to, the temptation will eventually become too great. When considering the *why* (such as *because I want to live into old age without clogged arteries or chemically induced nerve disorders from the junk inside this food*), putting down the box or never buying it in the first place makes a lot more sense. In fact, as we begin to think about things that are terrible for us in this way, we slowly rewire our brains toward different associations with these behaviors.

The same is true for things we want to do. We must have a strong *why* to get up in the morning and work on the projects we feel called to do. Then we will be much less likely to sleep in and waste the day away with things still left undone.

Logic may tell us that taking care of ourselves is the most important aspect of being happy; looking out for number one and making sure our own needs and desires are met seems like a perfectly logical path to success and happiness. But the National Institute on Aging has some interesting findings. The institute's director Dr. Robert Butler's research on the Blue Zones of the world shines a light on the people who live longer and healthier than the rest of us. It shows that feeling a sense of calling to purpose also correlates with longer lifespans and elevated feelings of happiness, especially when this purpose is linked to something or someone outside of oneself.

When you consider that it appears humans are actually happiest when caring for others, this seemingly backward type of logic that Christ taught in His sermons makes a lot of sense. The meek seem unlikely to inherit the earth and the last are never first in an earthly kingdom that champions doing whatever it takes to be first to the top. And as Dr. Joe Dispenza explains in his book *Breaking the Habit of Being Yourself*, modern quantum physicists' assertions that one can enter the quantum field of infinite possibilities by become no thing, in no time, in no place starts to sound a whole lot like dying to one's self to find the kingdom of heaven.

Learning to live life by loving God and loving people leads to experiencing moments of heaven on earth. Those moments stretch from minutes to hours and weeks, then eventually into a lifetime. David describes it beautifully in Psalm 27:4 as dwelling "in the house of the Lord all the days of my life." He's not simply focused on what happens after he dies, but on living in God's presence for the duration of this life.

If we all sought to live this way, what a heavenly place this earth could be. As we seek His ways, we rewire our brains—or as the Bible states it, we are "transformed by the renewing of our minds." We begin to hunger for the things that will bring us and others true joy and peace. We begin living with purpose as we dwell in the house of the Lord all the days of our lives.

Now, that's a great *why* to live for!

Food for Thought

- Do I believe my life is meant for goodness and love? What does this mean to me?
- Have I ever experienced moments of heaven on earth? How could this increase?
- How can I pray for God to transform my heart to experience heaven on earth?

Selah.

One Size Does Not Fit All

"Unless someone like you cares a whole lot, nothing's going to change. It's not."

—Dr. Seuss

Pear shaped, apple, hourglass. Ectomorph, mesomorph, endomorph. We all have different body types, all of which respond differently to environments, nutrition, and movement. If every person ate and exercised the exact same, we would still look different. Some people struggle to get into a state of health and wellbeing, while others seem to fall into it effortlessly.

Soil Check

People raised in health-conscious environments often maintain healthy lifestyles throughout their lives, but it doesn't guarantee they won't swing entirely in the opposite direction. Some may resent never having sugary or salty foods in their youth, devouring them with grins on their faces once they become adults who can eat whatever they choose.

The same can happen spiritually. Some people will come to know Christ as children and continue to live His teachings throughout their whole lives. Many of these people may grow up in what Jesus referred to as *healthy soil*, with parents who taught them Scriptures and modeled Christ-like behavior. Others may grow up outside of Christianity, but transform immediately after learning about Jesus and continue to grow in love and truth for the rest of their lives. While still others may experience transformation and soon revert back to tempting ways of living that the world advertises as the road to fulfillment. Some will take a while to allow Jesus to slowly make changes in their lives until they eventually realize they are completely transformed. Whatever the process may be for each person, it will surely look different from one human experience to another.

I think it is important to take into account how a person first came to learn about Christ. Was it as a child in Sunday school where they were given snacks and coloring books and told stories about Jesus? Were they sent to church as a punishment every time they were caught doing something wrong? Maybe some made an emotional decision to accept Christ at some event, while others thought about it for a long time before they finally felt ready. Regardless of where someone begins their faith journey, I think it is important to give each person the grace they need to grow from where they are.

I often feel I can relate to both types of Christian faith journeys. I began learning about God as a young girl brought up in Sunday school, then became a rebellious teen punished with church when I ran away from home. After that, I liked my church youth group so much that I became a goodie-two-shoes, afraid of the world as a bad and scary place. Later, I married young and became a wife who thought she did everything perfectly, then a divorcee who felt like she did it all wrong. From that point, I decided to walk away from anything related to God since I couldn't seem to get it right anyway. But I eventually grew to become a woman who could learn from all these experiences without judging anyone else's path as sinful.

God can use anything to draw someone near to Him. The path isn't always straight and narrow. Some of us step off the path—very far off the path—but God's grace is always there to fall back on. I heard a very wise monk call this grace *divine breath*, saying that as long as we still draw breath, we always have the opportunity to choose.

Flavorful Faith

I have a friend who loves hot sauce, the spicier the better. She was explaining about all the exciting types of spices she liked until one of our friends mentioned Tabasco. She said, "Ew! Not Tabasco, that's what we were punished with as kids. It was Tabasco on the tongue or soap in our mouths. I just can't do Tabasco!"

I couldn't help but think of how many people have an aversion to church because it was their equivalent to Tabasco punishment. Or those who feel like the church would be struck by lightning if they entered because they have always been told what horrible sinners they are, deciding they'd rather burn than bother with people waving "turn or burn" church signs.

This is where grace is of utmost importance for Christians who seek to bring lost and seeking hearts to a place of peace in Jesus. If someone can't stand your type of church, meet them where they are. If they hate Tabasco, bring them some Tapatio. Try another church, enjoy the beauty of God's creation in nature, or start meeting at a local coffee shop to create church together. After all, the Bible says that when two or more are gathered in Christ's name, He's there too.

There are as many ways of drawing near to God as there are people to do so. We must understand that no one's path will look the same, which is what makes the journey more beautiful. We come in all shapes and sizes, colors and personalities, so why would our journeys toward the Creator of all that diversity look exactly the same?

Racing to the Finish Line

I've known too many Christians who are so eager to get people to the finish line by saying the "sinner's prayer" that they forget to learn about those people and love them just as they are, just as God loves them.

Those of us who call ourselves followers of Christ might not always be the ones to bring people to know Him. We may never see the flowers bloom, but we can prepare the soil. Perhaps they've been hurt by modern so-called Christians that they've seen in our culture, perhaps they think they're simply unworthy of coming to God. In these cases, we must be willing to be patient gardeners and simply help prepare hearts to become ready to receive the good news that God loves them just as they are.

Don't think of it as being lukewarm or wishy-washy about the truth of the Bible, but simply knowing and being sensitive to what kind of soil we are dealing with. If the soil is dry, cracked, and hardened, we can till, water, and care for it. Too often, Christians just try to force a seed into dry and hardened ground. There is a season for plowing first. The soil needs a bit of love and nourishment before it can grow and reap a harvest from the planted seeds.

Regardless of where a person is in their journey or if they desire to come to church or know God, we are called to show them love out of genuine care for their souls. You may be the only exposure someone ever has to His message, so make sure it's a loving experience.

Food for Thought

- How did my childhood upbringing shape my ideas of Jesus, God, and church?
- Have I ever seen a Christian try to throw seeds at dry soil in someone's spiritual life? Have I ever done it myself?
- What is the condition of my heart? What would others say my heart is filled with?

Selah.

Part 3:
Junk Food Never Feeds the Soul

In her book *Eat Yourself Smart*, Dr. Caroline Leaf explains that Westerners have been transitioning away from consuming real food and replacing real nourishment with food-like products. We're turning to chips instead of potatoes, fruit snacks instead of fruits, and all the destructive qualities of sodas and other processed and packaged food-like products. These *foods* may satiate immediate feelings of hunger, but they've also left our society both malnourished and obese.

I can't help but wonder if we're also consuming soul-like-products for our spirits? Is our culture consuming pornography instead of intimacy with real individuals, social media instead of time with people in real environments? Are we seeking every possible product that promises enlightenment instead of sitting in stillness and asking our Creator to lead us closer to divine truth each day?

The following sections will explore what nourishes the soul. What soul-like products are we consuming that may seem pleasing for a moment, but leave our souls malnourished and lethargic? I am not sure I have the answers for these questions; however, my hope is that by asking the right questions and becoming still and aware enough to contemplate the answers, we will begin the process of positive change and spiritual growth through proper nutrition for our souls both individually and as a society.

SOUL FOOD

"It is not what goes into your mouth that defiles you; you are defiled by the words that come out of your mouth."

—Matthew 15:11, NLT

Google search the words *soul food*, and you will get an eyeful of fried chicken, corn bread, and macaroni and cheese. Another common description of comfort food is explained as food with high-calories and sugar, with simple preparation. Apparently, what brings comfort to Americans' souls is heartburn and acid reflux.

Heavenly Heartburn

As one of the many people in my generation to suffer from food allergies and stomach problems, I began to wonder why so-called *comfort food* always made me feel very *un*comfortable after eating it. Why don't we reserve the label for food that makes our bodies feel good, nourished, energized, or actually comfortable? I think of family members sitting around the Thanksgiving table after consuming portion sizes that could feed a small village, smiling, and saying, "Oh, it hurts so good!"

What is it about our culture that trains modern minds to think things that are terrible for our bodies are actually comforting? Can you think of ways mainstream culture trains us to believe that other terrible things will also make our souls feel good?

Sex sells, so watch the latest movie or TV series that will make you feel like your sex life is boring and obviously not as steamy and exciting as these on-screen romances. Perhaps you should go find a new one; a one-night stand sounds particularly fulfilling. Maybe just go it alone with the aid of pornography and avoid connecting with another human being altogether (just know you're wrecking your future prospects by training your brain to overindulge in copious and unnatural amounts of stimuli).

According to modern culture, we clearly need the newer cars, bigger houses, cuter outfits, latest gadgets, best perfumes, and more. Why? Because big business and great marketing campaigns tell us we do. Industries that make enormous amounts of money from our greed compete for our attention and our discretionary income, profiting from our insatiable desire for more. The question is: Do we really feel better after we have these things? Is this drive for chronic consumerism taking away our sadness and worries, making us happier, or leading to more fulfilled lives? Clearly not.

Perhaps different soul food can truly nourish the soul—another way. Maybe, *just maybe*, this way has been around for a very long time. And though it is full of sex and scandal, good, bad and ugly, it has not been marketed as *sexy*; it has not been marketed as what will fulfill. Perhaps it's been in the Bible all along.

Food for Thought

- What kind of soul-like products do I see people around me consuming? Which do I consume myself?
- How does mainstream culture affect what nourishes my soul?
- Do I make intentional choices about what I allow into my spirit?
- How have my experiences with church and society affected my ideas about the Bible?

Selah.

Bread of Life

"Jesus answered, 'It is written; Man shall not live on bread alone, but on every word that comes from the mouth of God.'"

—Matthew 4:4

The Bible is a mysterious text. Read it again and again, and its meaning can still completely elude you. Or read with an open and prayerful heart, and even the simplest of minds will see truth. These inspired Scriptures have stood the test of millennia. Though they were written thousands of years ago, truth still exists in the words today. When reading the Bible with an open and prayerful heart, each sitting can contain a range of experiences.

An Inspirational Text

The stories of the Bible are a great place to find inspiration in life and perspective about human nature and our propensity to do the wrong things over and over again, even when the right choice is so clearly presented to us. From spending time with the right people and walking

75

in integrity to diligently tackling the work we are called to, the Bible's wisdom teachings are full of practical advice even today.

The Scriptures are filled with poetry that seeks to invoke the depths of human feeling and emotion, inspiring life and drawing our hearts near to God's. The Bible's emotional poetry ranges from the erotic love described in Song of Solomon to the Psalmist's deepest depressions and highest joys. And then still the gospels focus on the good news of Christ coming to earth to teach us a new way to live in God that is full of grace and love. The rest of the commandments become quite redundant when we abide by what Jesus called the greatest commandment of loving God and loving people.

Sometimes we open the Bible and find profound truth that inspires our day or relates precisely to a situation we are going through, sometimes we read feeling like we're getting nothing as we struggle with the literal meaning of a scripture or why God would allow certain things.

I personally find new meaning in Scriptures that I have read dozens of times every time I open the text. When I am reading how God brought the Israelites out of slavery in Egypt, I see how He brought me out of my slavery under fear, bitterness, control, and a tendency toward depression. When I read about how He gave them water from a rock in the dessert, I see where He gave me the refreshment I so desperately needed during a tough season. And when God has made ways for me in situations that should have been impossible, I think of how He parted the Red Sea and made a way where there was none. It connects directly to my soul and comes alive in a more personal way.

Food for Thought

- How is the Bible both mysterious and straightforward?
- Do I believe the Bible is a "living Word?" What does that mean?
- What inspires life in me?
- In what ways does scripture inspire life in me?

Selah.

Acquired Tastes

"Salt is good, but if it loses its saltiness, how can it be made salty again?"

—Luke 14:34

Do you remember the first time you tried hard alcohol or a super sour candy? You probably didn't like it; you may have even made a face as the flavor rendered your taste buds half-numb.

Maybe you even pretended to like it to impress your friends. I remember I wanted to be cool, so I acted like I liked hard liquor, and now I wonder why. What is it about the dark side that makes us want to acquire a taste for something horrible for us? *Let me start to enjoy poisoning my body with sugar and alcohol. That sounds like a great idea!*

Taste Bud Trainer

I'm not against sugar or alcohol; in fact, I enjoy both on occasion. But I now realize how destructive they are to the cells in my body that refresh and make me feel great from day to day, so I do my best to keep them to a minimum these days. While plenty of other things can get us hooked, these are my two personal hang-ups. Yours may be different. Developing awareness of our good and destructive habits is as simple as bringing consciousness to what we consume, what we do, how we speak, and even how we think. Change starts with awareness.

When I consider some of the flavors our generation enjoys from sour candy to giant burgers, I often wonder if our ancestors would be absolutely disgusted with the foods our culture deems delicious. Would waxy licorice, sugary donuts, and greasy pizzas send their taste buds through the roof, or would they turn their noses at what we have done to food? Would they even call it food?

Simple Ingrediens

The modern slow cooking movement is focused on preparing and consuming foods more slowly with fresh ingredients to savor distinct flavors as they touch the pallet. This culinary movement both intrigues me and makes me feel saddened at how much excess sugar and salt fills our Western diets, making all other flavors hardly recognizable. So much of our nutrition has been watered down to bland nothingness, while companies add red dye and yellow 5 and all sorts of other chemicals to make the foods colorful once again. If their marketing research is successful, they'll do whatever it takes just to make the products desirable for sales to skyrocket.

I wonder what it would take to transition back to slower food, healthier ingredients, and slower lifestyles that actually help digest these foods better? Realizing that food-like products are not food may be a start; making a conscious effort to become more aware of how we treat the bodies we have for our entire lives might be wise. Regardless of the method people choose to take better care of themselves, it all starts with awareness.

I'm not talking about grinding our spiritual grains in a stone pot or anything, but getting back to basics with the aid of modern conveniences and technology. We could go back to this kind of spiritual nutrition with foreknowledge of the pitfalls that the generations before us unfortunately never knew. Before we think about that, let's examine for a moment that we are not the first generation to process and genetically modify our spirituality.

In Jesus' day, the Pharisees were adding all kinds of their own poisonous ingredients to religion and leaving out the most nutritional contents like God's love and grace for His people. Jesus equated the extra rules and philosophy that the religious leaders of the day added to religion as yeast—starting small but soon permeating everything and changing the original message of God's goodness for His people.

78

The good news is that we can go back. We see God throughout scripture constantly calling His children to come back to Him even after they had turned away time and time again. We see He continued to bring them back into the original dignity they were created for, even after humanity basically said, *No thank you; that seems a bit scary and complicated,* time and time again.

How much of our faith and spirituality has been watered down or over-processed into such unrecognizable goop that we have to add our own spiritual chemicals? Have we taken the nutrition out of a spiritual life and substituted it with white bread? Do we add extra ingredients like Pharisees adding and emphasizing man-made rules that God never outlined in the first place? Or by adding eccentric and strange practices that prove we have been "moved by the Spirit?" What might a spiritual life look like if we went back to the basic nourishing ingredients that our ancestors started with?

Food for Thought

- What food or drink have I developed a taste for? Is it good for me? Why did I decide to acquire that taste?
- Have I developed a taste for over-processed foods? If so, do I actually like them or it is just what's socially available?
- How may I have done the same in my spiritual life? Have I acquired a taste for something or socially conformed to a bland soul-like spirituality?
- How have modern Christians become like the Pharisees of Jesus time, potentially including myself? What might returning to God's original design look like?

Selah.

More Than Just Morals

"Love the Lord your God with all your heart and with all
your soul and with all your mind… and love your neighbor as
yourself. All the Law and the Prophets hang on these two
commandments."

—Matthew 22:37–40

Is it good to have a healthy moral compass? Of course! Is it nice to
impose our moral code on everyone around us? Not so much. People
tend to be so caught up in who is wrong and who is right that they
miss the whole point of communing with God.

Jesus laid it out for us pretty straightforward. Love God and
love the people He's created; everything else will fall into place. Think
about it, if you love God and others, you're not going to murder people
or commit adultery with their spouses. If you love God and others,
you won't covet what they have but be happy for them because you
love them. All things fall naturally into place when we act out of love.

When we focus our efforts on righteousness defined as right
relationship with both God and others, the morals fall into place. If I
desire to remain in right relationship to you, I am not going to seek to
violate you in any way. The same goes for if I want to remain in right
relationship with God. To remain in right relationship with someone,
we desire to do what is good for them, what is pleasing, and what is
right. When we are being loving, there is little desire to do wrong to
ourselves or another human being. The rules become unimportant, not
because they cease to be followed, but because we naturally follow
them when we are loving.

I'm Right; You're Wrong

For thousands of years, cultures have been clashing with each other,
nations warring against nations, and religions against religions—killing
each other over who is right and who is wrong, all the while missing
the point. The pride of trying to prove who has the best brand of
religion has caused society to leave God entirely out of the equation.
With all the effort of trying to prove our own right-ness, we have

completely missed the righteousness of being in right relationships with God and others. We have neglected to love God or others, all for the sake of being right, which obviously makes us all so incredibly wrong.

Religious people of Jesus' day would try to prove how right they were by attempting to trick Him into saying the wrong things so they could condemn Him. (Look how little we've changed!) How often do we see this today with people using religion to condemn others? It is the very nature we succumb to when we identify with the clay we were formed from rather than the breath we were inspired to live through. We see people all throughout scripture and history declare that their own ways are right for the sake of their own desires.

But we also see God throughout scripture and history calling His people back into relationship with Him, to return to the reason He created them at the start. Time after time, the human race has rejected the divinity that was inspired from the beginning and instead settled for something closer to the lump of clay we were made from. Though humanity continued to settle for the most basic of instincts as opposed to the God-breathed divinity we were created for, God continued to reach out and give guidelines for how to return to this original dignity He so longed to give back. The rebellious nature of the human heart tends to reject rules, even ones that lead to our benefit, safekeeping, and wellbeing.

When we fight over whose brand of religion is correct—whose beliefs are right—we miss the whole point. When we are trying so hard to be moral and do the right things, we may find every loophole possible to still keep the rules without actually doing what is loving and good.

Healthy vs. Fit

When I first became a fitness trainer in 2003 at Gold's Gym, I was a Pharisee of trainers. Like the ancient religious leaders focused on spiritual appearances, my main concern for my clients and myself was what we would look like. We wanted to look fit, and we'd take whatever the fastest route was to get there. I remember drinking diet drinks full of illegal ephedra, taking diet pills (which I am sure contributed to my stomach problems down the line), lifting weights, and doing cardio until I nearly passed out. I looked how I wanted to look (maybe even slightly more like the Incredible Hulk than I may have preferred), but I didn't get there in a way that was beneficial to my body long-term. I looked fit, but I was not healthy.

As I grew as a fitness instructor and a person, I began to incorporate a more holistic approach to life and to fitness. I began to realize that if I made my clients and myself healthy, looking amazing would naturally follow. I began focusing more on healthy food choices and more enjoyable forms of exercise to bring us into a healthier state of being from the inside out. I racked up seven different certifications in everything from Pilates to Russian kettlebells and read everything about health and longevity that I could get my hands on.

Moralistic Christianity (or any religion, for that matter) can be a lot like striving to look fit without first becoming healthy. Like my experience as a young trainer, this kind of thinking can actually deteriorate the state of our spiritual health if all we focus on is morality. Just as looking amazing is a side effect of a healthy and enjoyable nutrition and exercise routine, living morally is a natural side effect of a healthy spirit pursing love, abundant life, and a transformation of the heart.

You may look healthy for a while after taking diet pills, over-exercising, or getting liposuction, but none of these things will ultimately make you healthy. Moralistic living and following all the rules without a transformed heart has a similar effect. The only people Jesus spoke to harshly were hyper-religious people like the Pharisees. He constantly told the religious leaders of the day who thought they had it right because they were following all the rules that they actually got it all wrong because their hearts were still ugly and full of judgment.

In diet and exercise, it is important to first seek health, then rejoice when we see our bodies changing from the inside out. The same is true for spirituality. We must first seek a transformed heart: to be more loving like Christ, seeking justice for the oppressed, caring for the earth He created, and rejoicing when we also begin to behave in ways that choose wisdom and benefit our lives and the world around us in kind. The other way may work for a while but will never ultimately fulfill, and it almost always eventually destroys what started out healthy in the process.

Choosing Our Identity

There is so much beauty in remembering all the way back to the beginning of the story when God breathed His own life into the man, creating him to be such a beautiful and mysterious cross between heaven and earth. Although we are earthly, fleshly beings, we can remember that as long as we still live, we always have a choice. We can choose to live more in our heavenly identity or our earthly one.

Most people will remain primarily in their earthly identity, while others will oscillate from one to the other throughout their lifetimes. Some will take what Jesus calls the narrow path to heaven that very few will find, and we may call these the *saints*. Whatever you wish to call them, a few will choose to live in their heavenly identity more of the time, which makes them able to recognize this same identity in others, to see God's inspiration in others and in everything around them.

When we see and experience God in everything, we begin to truly live life in a way that makes His kingdom and His will the same on earth as it is in heaven, in a way that heaven can be known on earth, here in this lifetime and into the next.

Food for Thought

- What does it mean to be loving?
- How can loving God and loving people lead me to follow every other commandment?
- How might seeking to change my heart transform my will to be more like God's better than if I just try to follow all the rules?
- In what ways do I identify more with a lump of clay (being *only human*), and in what ways to I identify with being inspired (or *breathed into*) by the Spirit of God?

- Do I tend to have a rebellious heart or one that seeks the greatest truth and good? How can I be sure?

Selah.

Sticky-Sweet Pride

"Humble yourselves before the Lord, and He will
lift you up."

—James 4:10

What is the junk food among junk foods? Is it trans fats? Starchy carbs? Excess sodium?

I think refined sugar has probably received the worst rap of them all; in my own research, it seems to be the most harmful, particularly in excess. As a society, we have been conditioned to think sugar tastes good—the sweeter the better—and that sugar is a treat. Yet research shows us that refined sugar breaks down the cells in our body, is as addictive as cocaine, and causes a host of nasty symptoms ranging from acne and cellulite to diabetes and cancer.

Pride Comes Before a Fall

If I had to choose a refined sugar of the soul, I think it would be pride. Like sugar, pride can take a more natural form, such as taking pride in a job well done, or a refined form like considering yourself to be better than everyone else.

Ethnocentrism is defined as judging another culture solely by the values and standards of one's own culture. Ethnocentric groups tend to view their culture as superior, looking down on those who are not like them as inferior. When I think of most societies of the world today, they tend to be conditioned to be proud of themselves, their countries, and their accomplishments with higher confidence in how their own people live.

None of these things are particularly bad, but when a confident culture turns into a culture of narcissists who think they are better than everyone else, this is where pride seems to turn more processed and refined. Due to this inherent pride in our human clay-like nature, we tend to view ourselves as perfect and everyone else as problematic. We fail to recognize that our own self-made idols have made us feel secure and important in an echo chamber of our own sin—telling us we are hitting the mark, when in fact we have missed the target. Our pride blinds us.

Humility at Heart

We could be doing all the things that make us look good: helping people, having a strong moral code, and being nice to people to their face, all the while having a bitter and hateful heart, considering others to be far below us. I think how often I hear "good people" express hatred and badmouth other people groups. I usually hear this from people who actually love others but are being influenced in our society that makes it sound cool, independent, angsty, or smarter.

We are called to be humble servants. Although we can surely take pride in doing things well, it is possible to avoid being pride*ful* about how amazing we are to be able to do those things. We can joyfully do all things without making all things about us. Christ said that what we do for the least of people we are doing for Him.

We have had it backward. We worship beauty, wealth, intimacy, feeling loved and adored. Though all of those things are amazing, they become toxic when we forget that they are all gifts to enjoy and share with the world around us. Humbly recognizing God's hand of favor and provision in our lives, we can be more freely generous as we recognize how generous He has been with us. Though people, finances, and outer beauty may change or fail us, God will never fail us.

Like the sugar that seems to be hidden in just about every food item on the market today, pride can often be so easily hidden in even the best of intentions. How will I look if I do that? What will they think if I say this? Maybe they will notice if I donate to that. Did anyone see how much I put in the tithing basket?

The false self is always competing for a way to feel important and special, forgetting the original dignity of the true self, made in God's image that is already more important and special than we can realize. If we think of taking pride in doing in a job well done like eating natural fruit sugar versus the pride of trying to be someone we are not like eating the added sugar in a tub of licorice, we can start to recognize that, although the unit may be the same, a measure of pride makes the outcome and nutritional effect very different.

Food for Thought

- In what ways do I take pride in what I do?
- In what ways am I prideful? (If you're having difficulty, consider the ways others are prideful, then reflect inward.)
- How might my life and others around me reflect back things I need to recognize in myself?

Selah.

The Narrow Path

"The soul has been given its own ears to hear things the mind does not understand."

—Rumi

Might there be another entry point into spirituality than social conditioning and succumbing to our prideful false self? Can we reach for something deeper and more mysterious than could ever be explained or really understood by the intellect at all?

Literally Loving

Friar Richard Rohr explains that the Enlightenment period of history is wrongly named because society actually stepped backward, considering everything literally and leaving no room for very real spiritual and emotional thought.

Some things must be experienced by the soul; indeed, many things that are very real cannot be measured or touched. We push these things away because they are not tangible or measurable, they seem dangerous in a way, not safe—things such as love, vulnerability with others, or sacrificing one's self.

There is something so life-giving and freeing about it all, but allowing mysterious and unknown answers in our lives can feel counterintuitive when we have been conditioned to be enlightened by our controlled understanding of things. To be vulnerable and truly love and to figuratively hold your heart in front of another person with the ability to smash it in their hands, believing they won't destroy it, causes fear in the bravest of hearts. Yet to be vulnerable and allow space for the possibility of both pain and bliss is the only way to experience life more abundantly alongside the other beautiful souls we are blessed to experience this life with.

As C.S. Lewis says in *The Four Loves*: "To love at all is to be vulnerable. Love anything, and your heart will be wrung and possibly broken. If you want to make sure of keeping it intact, you must give it to no one, not even an animal. Wrap it carefully round with hobbies and little luxuries; avoid all entanglements. Lock it up safe in the casket or coffin of your selfishness. But in that casket, safe, dark, motionless, airless, it will change. It will not be broken, it will become unbreakable, impenetrable, irredeemable. To love is to be vulnerable."

Well-Made Creations

Walking in the loving, soul-nourishing, life-changing mystery that Christ came to teach us about is sometimes a scary and narrow road that few will find. It cannot be bought into like some get-rich-quick scheme that'll give you a grand prize if you sign up five of your friends. Instead, we must strip away all door prizes and acknowledgments, all the silly images we have defined ourselves by, and strip ourselves down to humility. We are so precious in the eyes of God that there is no sense in arguing about who's right or wrong; these things only distract us from living in God's love.

The church was not meant to be some beautiful or plain place where someone comes to *get some God*. Our very bodies are meant to be the container for God's divine breath, giving life that reflects the very divinity of God.

We are created in His image, yet we belittle ourselves and others when we put on false identities of intelligence, beauty, and success. What we fail to realize is that we already are all of those things, if we would simply drop the mask.

Food for Thought

- In what ways do I take life too literally? Can I make space for intangible feelings and experiences?
- What barriers have I put up in my own life through fear of love and vulnerability?
- What do I fear about opening up completely to other people?
- In what ways do I wear a mask? What would happen if I dropped the mask?
- What would happen if I was vulnerable with myself and others?

Selah.

Diets Don't Work

"He refreshes my soul. He guides me along the right path for His name's sake."

—Psalm 23:3

I hope that our culture is beginning to realize that diets don't work and that starving our brains of necessary fats and calories is just plain wrong. It is my hope that the collective consciousness that has bought into this lie is coming to an awareness that adopting lifestyles that include proper amounts of healthy fats, grains, fruits, vegetables, and proteins will give us the energy we need to think clearly and move energetically throughout our lives.

Avoiding Spiritual Starvation

If you have ever tried a fad diet, you may be very familiar with the feeling of brain fog and lethargy that comes from consuming such an imbalanced diet. The same can be true when it comes to spirituality. Sometimes we can get so excited about praise and worship that we neglect to be of any service to anyone, or so pumped about serving the church and participating in different projects that we forget to slow down and spend intimate time with God to refresh our souls, or even spend so much time in prayer and silence that we neglect the world around us altogether—forgetting the second half of the "love God, love people" equation.

If it makes sense that our bodies cannot survive without proper nutrition and that they do not thrive when fed inadequate nutrients, would it not also make sense that our souls would require the same attention?

Food for Thought

- Has my soul been on a diet, becoming too thin to be healthy?
- Is my soul full of the nourishing fruits of love, joy, peace, patience, kindness, goodness, faithfulness, gentleness, and self-control?

Selah.

Foundational Foods

"Don't worry about anything; instead, pray about everything.
Tell God what you need, and thank Him for all He
has done."

—Philippians 4:6

A balanced spiritual diet relies on a few food groups, like prayer, meditation, reading God's Word, and community with people of a similar faith. Different people, however, will consume these nutrients, in different ways.

We can choose to get our daily dose of vitamin C from an orange or from broccoli, or perhaps from both, but we're consuming vitamin C regardless. Similarly, one person's prayer life may be quiet and contemplative, while another is more comfortable speaking aloud with God in group prayer. One person may feel comfortable in a large church, while another prefers a small, intimate setting.

Come Just as You Are

When it comes to prayer, some people pray by speaking or writing their conversations with the Lord. Waiting quietly for His answers may sound a bit intangible to wrap our heads around; however, it often feels something like a stirring peace in our hearts moving us toward a certain decision or another.

The Bible says that we grow stronger as we wait upon the Lord, and when we are weak, He is strong and near to the brokenhearted. As we come to Him with our brokenness, our weaknesses, and all our troubled thoughts of anxiety and depression, we can trust that He will begin to work on us right where we are. Even when we are full of doubts, worries, or sadness, we can come to God in those places.

We do not have to clean ourselves up before we come to God, He sees us just as we are. We don't need to hide, and He doesn't want us to. He will make us strong, peaceful, healed, and whole if we will reach out to Him and let Him do the work. This may take time and patience, but the wholeness of God is worth the wait. The process is rarely once and for all. There will be many times in our lives when we will come to God broken and unfulfilled and must wait on His healing once again.

Food for Thought

- What prayers have I been waiting for answers from God? Is it making me stronger?
- In what ways can I come to God in my brokenness with an expectant heart that He will make me stronger?

Selah.

Rest and Restoration

"Come to Me, all you who are weary and burdened, and I will
give you rest."

—Matthew 11:28

Coming to God in our brokenness can be harder than it seems because it requires an amount of humility and surrender that few possess. Society as a whole does not praise or recommend setting aside our pride or giving up control of a situation—quite the opposite. Secular teaching says we're masters of our universe, which is only partly true at best. Whether we know it or not, God's Spirit is what gives us creativity to use how we please. He made us creative, thinking beings inspired by His Spirit to be co-creators in this beautiful world He continues to create with us.

But we can use this power of co-creation for good or for evil. We can choose to build up or to destroy. This is where laying down our desire to control it all and seeking God's expert advice as Creator of the universe becomes imperative.

Simple Surrender

God often uses foolish things of the world to do incredible things for His kingdom. He uses things that seem to make absolutely no sense so that we know His hand was in them, often turning our notions of what is beneficial and desirable on their heads. When we come to Him admitting our weakness, brokenness, fears and anxieties, we leave His presence healed by simply surrendering to His way in us.

Surrender is simple but not easy. Surrender goes against everything in us that seeks to control. When we give up control and put our lives in the hands of our good Creator, we often are amazed by what He will do with our lives. It may feel a bit like a rollercoaster at times, but instead of being terrified of the rollercoaster, life can be so much more enjoyable when we throw our hands up, let out a loud shout and enjoy the ride.

Food for Thought

- Do I consider myself a humble person? Do others?
- What areas of my life do I try to control?
- How might I benefit by surrendering them to God?

Selah.

Part 4:
It Might Be Time for a Detox

My personal life motto has long been that I desire to be so present in every moment of life that it is as if I have lived a thousand lifetimes. Yet when life's tasks pile on, we can easily get caught up in the minutia of what we think needs to be done rather than savoring the experiences that our lives have to offer. This is when self-care care just doesn't quite cut it; we need what I call *soul-care*.

Whereas the body can sometimes benefit best from a bodily reset that fasting or detoxifying can deliver, sometimes the souls needs the reset that a retreat or simply a day away from the responsibilities of life can give. Both our bodies and souls can only continue to function properly for so long without taking the proper rest, restoration, and rejuvenation that God's true presence provides. So, let's start considering the signs.

That Spiritual Bellyache Won't Go Away

"I have come that you may have life, and have it
more abundantly."

—John 10:10

Years ago, my friend's mother bought an ionic foot detox machine that she was so excited to try on us. I started out highly skeptical but stayed open-minded as we gave it a go. I suffered from chronic allergies and sinus infections, and her son had just returned from a remote stint in Afghanistan, where food scarcity left him and his fellow soldiers resorting to grabbing chickens from the local village and frying them in cans of ammunition—leaving him exposed to large amounts of heavy metals, to say the least.

I politely acquiesced as she instructed us to soak our feet in the tubs of water and saline solution then proceeded to strap our wrists to

93

the machine for about a half hour, explaining that the water would change colors based on the types of toxins being pulled from our bodies. Within minutes, the water started turning nasty swirls of greens and brown. Then astonishingly, small bits of metal began floating around in my friend's water, like one of those toys that moves tiny iron flakes around with a magnet, as my tub filled with snotty swap-looking bubbles of mucous-like substances.

How did this machine know he was full of heavy metals and I was full of allergens? I was sold. Since then, as I've continued to foot detox from time to time over the years, I have seen less mucous and experienced fewer sinus allergy problems on the whole.

Why tell the story of a disgusting but effective detoxification? Because sometimes our bodies and souls need cleansing beyond just plenty of drinking water and regular exercise. Whether it's because someone is just beginning to bring awareness to their health after living a toxic life for a long time or because a specific event has been extra toxic to their body or soul, a soul detox can sometimes be necessary.

Breaking the Distraction Addiction

I generally eat pretty healthfully, allowing myself a little indulgence now and then so that I don't end up craving it like crazy later. There have been times, however, when I have allowed small things to creep into my diet one at a time until they eventually add up to a giant lifestyle change. It usually starts when I go on holiday or decide to "live a little" and eat whatever I want for a while—whatever sounds good at the moment, whatever I haven't had in a long time. After a few days of this (or weeks if I'm home with family), I develop a sort of permanently bloated feeling. It's uncomfortable and unsightly and makes me feel gassy and gross. If only I could remember the awful aftermath before I started to eat some of these things.

It's around this time that I usually decide to do some sort of detox. Slowly making poor choices becomes addictive for me, so I personally have to completely eradicate the possibility of making those choices for a period of time in order to break the addiction. Likewise, fasting for spiritual reasons also helps detox the body, spirit, and mind.

We can experience a spiritual bellyache when our souls start to become filled with bad decisions and habitual disobedience. This is when I find it helpful to take a fast from behaviors, as well. Every year, I fast from social media for at least 40 days to detox from my neurotic habit of checking how many people liked my latest post or from constantly swiping through to mindlessly like what all my friends are posting. In the past, I've also fasted from dating, from swearing, from sugar on weekdays, and from eating anything other than vegetables. I will fast from just about anything that might distract me, especially when I am focused on a task I feel is particularly important (like writing a book that God put on my heart).

The point of a fast is to get our focus off the thing we are fasting *from* and instead drawing our attention to God and what He is calling us *to*. When first bringing fasting into your spiritual lifestyle, I suggest focusing completely on the point of your fast rather than on what you've given up. Over time and much practice through many fasts, I have found that focus and revelation are sure to come.

My relationship with food has changed a lot since my brother's death. Before, I could hardly skip a meal, let alone fast for a day or more, but after I involuntarily stopped eating for a month after his death, going without food really doesn't bother my stomach all that much. What does get bothered is my constant need for distraction. It is amazing how many times I've reached for something to eat out of a desire to distract my mind, out of boredom per se, even though I was not even hungry.

Sometimes I don't truly feel God speak until the second or third day of a food fast. Is it simply delusion from hunger pangs? I've studied materials on intermittent fasting from several different people, including nutritionist Dr. Oz Garcia's *Is Intermittent Fasting for You,* which explain that periods of fasting have actually been shown to increase brain function.

During a fast, it is much clearer to see that my mind is searching for places to go to avoid stillness, meditation, and seeking God. But once the monkey mind is at rest, which usually takes a couple days to settle after giving up my current distraction or vice of choice, I become still enough to hear God speak. At first, it may seem like imagination, wishful thinking or just plain nothing, but I believe as we practice hearing God's voice, we will begin to recognize it more and more. He speaks in a still, small voice, and when we get quiet and still enough to hear it, our lives are enriched.

Tapping into Stillness and Awareness

When we develop small habits of destruction, whether to our body or to our soul, it can often take a drastic measure or some sort of reset to get ourselves pointed in the direction we wish to head. Whether it is with food or with the spirit, it is beneficial to develop the kind of self-awareness that recognizes when we have wandered into a territory that no longer serves us.

In James Martin's book *Becoming Who You Are*, he relays a story about Trappist monk Thomas Merton's struggle with having an intimate relationship with a nurse after having taken his vow of celibacy. Although he tried to hide it at first, his abbot went on to describe that when someone breaks one of their vows, it often leads to breaking all the others. In his case, breaking his celibacy also led to breaking obedience, fidelity to monastic life, and stability. We rarely create just one habit. Our habits, for better or worse, tend to have a domino effect that spreads quickly to other parts of our lives.

This reminds me of how sometimes we can "blow our diet," so to speak, and go on to keep eating junk for the rest of the day because we feel like the day is already ruined. Or more often, it's like having an occasional soda, which slowly turns into the habit of drinking a soda a day.

Developing awareness of the ways that we create destructive habits and creating ways to turn those habits back around is a far more spiritually nourishing way to live than to apathetically give into our habits and decide it's just the way we are. God created us beautifully, wonderfully, and so very good. When we seek to return to being as close to God's original design as we are capable, we begin to live more content and fulfilled lives.

I hope we all learn to slow down and be still enough to hear His voice in our lives, whatever means that may come by. That we become free of the burdens of our most destructive habits and experience peace in the present moment that God has for us here and now. That we start to believe without a doubt that God cares for our future, so we can stop mentally running into future moments with worry and miss the wonder of the only moment we will truly ever have: the one we are fully present in, right now.

Soul Cleanse

How do we detoxify our souls? There are many ways to do this, including and not limited to meditation, taking time to rest, and getting away from the stresses of everyday life. My personal spiritual detox of choice is visiting monasteries.

My favorite monastery is the New Camaldoli Hermitage. New Camaldoli is a silent retreat tucked into the Santa Lucia Mountains of Big Sur, California. Cell phone coverage drops off about an hour before I arrive, at which point nothing can come between me and the silent bliss that awaits. Soaring cliffs hold me close on one side, and seemingly endless ocean seas beckon me from the other. I feel the weight of the world falling away as the wind blows through my ponytail, my hands grip the steering wheel of my tiny blue convertible, and I smile.

The first time I visited this particular monastery, I listened to Bessel Van der Kolk's book *The Body Keeps The Score* during the drive, which laid a foundation for the kind of healing that God had in store for me on that particular trip. *The Body Keeps The Score* is about how traumatic memories are stored in our bodies and traumatized people often reactively respond to situations despite logically wanting to act differently. The way our bodies recollect the chemical pathways happens as neurons fire in a certain way that we are often unaware of until we find ourselves stuck in the same patterns again and again. The beauty of this neuro-scientific discovery is that these pathways can be changed.

On this visit, I focused on more deeply healing from the death of my brother than I had previously been able to process. Though my brother and I were best friends when he died, I remembered feeling incredibly remorseful for how I'd treated him when we were little kids. Since I knew this line of thinking was illogical, I'd pushed it from my mind at the time of his passing. We had been best friends our entire lives, so why would I suddenly regret the times I was a total brat to him as a baby? He'd never held it against me, and it was really just part of being little kids growing up together, so I pushed it aside and never thought about it again until several years later in the silence of my tiny room in the monastery.

Pouring my feelings onto the pages of the journal in front of me, the tears began to flow—releasing pain of a life lost so young, words left unsaid, and things left undone. Feelings about my brother, our friendship, his life, his death, and my regrets for any time I treated him less than he deserved spilled out of me like a shaken bottle uncorked. It was illogical and I knew it, but it was something I desperately needed to process, something my body and mind still held onto.

So, I wrote about it, cried about it, and finally let it go. I left the monastery lighter and freer than I was when I had arrived. I left detoxed of the junk in my spirit like sludge in the arteries of my freedom in Christ, in my ability to live without condemnation and to live in love and grace with myself and others...to live life more abundantly.

Falling Upward

Spiritual detoxes are cleansing and refreshing in a way that is simply beyond description, as much as I may try. With time and practice, we don't need to wait for a designated spiritual retreat to cleanse the soul.

Just as a person who has already detoxified physically can now choose to eat a nutritionally sound diet that naturally keeps the body in harmony, we can learn over time how to naturally keep the soul in harmony. Of course, things may slip in and get us off track from time to time just like they can in our diets; however, the more often we return to center in the nutrition of both our body and soul, the more likely we are to remain there for longer periods of time.

As we grow and deepen our spiritual lives over time, the need for a major retreat to get back to center becomes less crucial, though no less enjoyable. As we mature in our spirit, we are able to make micro adjustments; we fall upward, so to speak. The major things that used to trip us up do not faze us any longer, and we notice the small things that take us off track, making adjustments more quickly and easily. Just as a person with a fitness routine they have maintained for the better part of a decade finds it much easier to get back into the routine after a week of vacation than a person just starting out, the spiritual life becomes a beautiful ritual that integrates into daily life, infusing it with energy, vitality, and greater ease to return to.

I hope we all learn to slow down and be still enough to hear His voice in our lives, by whatever means. That we become free of the burdens of our most destructive habits and experience peace in the present moment that God has for us here and now. That we start to believe without a doubt that God cares for our future, so we can stop mentally running into future moments with worry and missing the wonder of the only moment we will truly ever have: the one we are fully present in, right now.

Food for Thought

- Which spiritually nourishing habits could I create to replace the poor ones?
- What ways do I tend to distract myself from self-reflection or from stillness in the present moment?
- Am I at a spiritual point where my soul needs a major detox, or am I good at making the micro adjustments necessary to remain in spiritual balance?

Selah.

Same Old Sin

"As far as the east is from the west, that is how far He has removed our transgressions from us."

—Psalm 103:12

It seems I fall into the same old sin over and over again. And it always seems to be when I think I am immune to it that I fall the hardest. I have often felt unworthy of coming to God when I have fallen short of what I know is best, yet He reminds me in His Word and by His Spirit that I am no more or less worthy than at the moment I messed up. I am no more or less His child, His beloved, His creation when I am missing the mark or hitting it.

God's Got Me

It's taken a long time for my stubborn spirit to really understand and accept this truth. I always felt like I wasn't good enough for the people in my life, let alone God. So, I'd replay this cycle like a broken record, subconsciously looking for situations that felt familiar with people I worried I could never please. I would act as if I were lucky they saw something in me at all and hope they could not see my past, my mistakes, and my disqualifications—projecting my insecurities by the way I clung to anyone who would value me in even the slightest way.

God would continue to work in me through these fears and doubts, reminding me not to hold onto the guilt of past mistakes because He's made me a new creation. Eventually, I'd forget His mercies toward me and become arrogant in my ability to be the good girl, convincing myself I was immune to remaking my same mistakes. But I was being good for the wrong reasons. Soon enough, I'd fall right back into my same old patterns, continuing the cycle of guilt, shame, repentance, and acceptance. Until I eventually ditched my arrogant *I got this* mentality for a humble confidence that actually God's got me.

God still reminds me that He loves me either way, that my good choices will benefit my life and those around me, and yet He still has so much grace even for my bad choices. He continues to love me, use me, and work all things together for my good in spite of them. He reminds me that He sees my heart to keep trying to reach Him and that He chooses not to see my failures or weaknesses. He reminds me that even when I am weak, He is strong, and He comes to work in each situation when I ask. Once I've surrendered even my worst mistakes and humbly come to Him for help, He turns them around for my good and helps me live in a way that benefits my body, mind, and spirit, as well as those around me.

Boundaries and Benefits

God didn't create rules and laws just to spoil all our fun. Like a good parent sets boundaries for their own children to avoid injury or death, He created boundaries for the safety of our bodies, minds, and souls.

Just think about the potential consequences of sex. Nobody needs the potential grief of wondering who's the baby daddy or if they should keep it. God doesn't want our lives to end up looking like a mild version of the Jerry Springer show, which is why his boundaries create situations where pregnancy is something to celebrate. His ideal is for us to feel safe in a loving relationship and enjoy a lifetime of caring for a child in partnership, rather than struggling to do it as a single parent on our own.

He also has incredible amounts of grace for when we do get ourselves into less than ideal situations. He has hope for us even when we fall again and again, and He extends a hand to pick us back up. God called His people to be lenders rather than borrowers, but we see today how massive amounts of debt leaves people crushed under the weight of the things they own. And we are called to treat our bodies as temples so that we can live out our days in joy, rather than meeting an early fate because of blocked arteries or overdoses.

In his book *The Blue Zones*, author Dan Buettner documents the longest-living populations in the world, denoted as "blue zones" on a map, who have shown to live several years beyond the world average. Interestingly, the only blue zone in America is a group of Seventh Day Adventist Christians in Loma Linda, California, who live their lives strictly according to biblical principles. Their sense of community, physical activity, and nutrition are all based on Old Testament principals, and they live longer for it—the longest in the U.S., in fact. I'm not saying we need to give up bacon or start living like it's the first century, but it may be worthwhile to examine our lives in the mirror of what God laid out as an ideal to see if we might be happier and perhaps even live a bit longer for it.

Making it Right

My favorite definition of the word *righteousness* is "right relationship." When we live in a right relationship with God, others, and ourselves we are truly living by what Jesus called the greatest commandments of loving God with all our heart and loving our neighbors as ourselves. The beautiful thing about seeking right relationships is that, by bringing God into these relationships, He can turn even the sourest relationships sweet.

I have seen this in my own life with family members I never thought I would be able to tolerate, much less truly love and enjoy spending time together. I thought there was too much trauma and hoped to just be civil one day, yet God had a right relationship in mind for us. Having right relationships with God, others, and ourselves is the most beautiful definition of righteousness that I can imagine. If only we could start with righteous soul relationships with God, in our homes, and in our communities, perhaps righteousness would spread to the world around us.

Bringing our lives into alignment with God's Word and walking in righteousness will not always be a linear path. Even while writing this book, I fell into old patterns that broke right relationships with God, others, and myself—much like Paul describes as a thorn in his side. When I came back to writing the next day, I wrote to God in my prayer journal that I was not worthy to ask for His help and inspiration. He gently reminded me, *Do you think you were completely righteous before? Do you think I love and cherish you any less as my child now?*

There is a mysterious balance between faith and works, between obedience and unearned grace. Grace is not an excuse to sin but every reason to forgive ourselves and others, then strive to live better and more abundantly.

Food for Thought

- Do my choices make me feel happy and fulfilled in life?
- Can I forgive myself and others for the places we miss the mark in our lives and start fresh?
- Can I think of ways I live in right relationship?
- What personal relationships could I bring to God to be made better?

Selah.

102

We Get What We Put In

"Death and life are in the power of the tongue, and those who love it will eat its fruits."

—Proverbs 18:21

Although we all have different needs and require different nutritional staples to maintain a balanced lifestyle, we also know none of us needs an excess of starchy, processed carbohydrates and refined sugars in our diets. The same goes for certain thoughts and behaviors. For too long, Western culture's marketing industries have convinced us that if we can't believe it's not butter, then the homogenized oil must be much better for our bodies. Do a little research, though, and you will quickly learn that these substances are much more harmful to the body than the butter ever could be. Culture is beginning to clue in to the fact that truly healthy foods don't need advertisements claiming to be healthy.

Pulling Weeds, Sewing Seeds, and Seeing Fruit

It's the same for healthy lifestyles. Sex may sell, but a string of broken relationships will sell your soul at a severely discounted price. The beer commercial promising you will be just as fit and fun as its actors may look appealing, but waking up with a beer gut and a hangover actually puts us much farther from that illusion than before all the drinks. Taking that payday loan may seem like a great solution for the moment, but when the time comes to actually pay up, where's the easy solution? I am not saying sex, beer, or money are bad. Not at all. But all things in their proper time and context. Ice cream in itself is not inherently bad, but if you eat a gallon before bed every night, chances are you won't like the results.

If you've ever had to take a round of antibiotics or detoxed very thoroughly, you may know how important it is to replace your gut's natural flora with good bacteria. Similarly, living a life of bad choices can sometimes lead to uncomfortable consequences— financial troubles, high stress, utter despair, and any number of maladies. It is important not just to detox, but also to replenish our spirit with good nutrients such as joy, love, peace, and patience.

Easier said than done. These are characteristics that we often need to experience inside ourselves before we can live them out. Unfortunately, we live in a time when people make fun of each other as a way to relate and connect, often telling jokes that put down themselves or others. This leaves little room for life-giving, spirit-building words of praise—so much so that it can seem awkward when we do say uplifting things to one another.

I encourage you to start with yourself. Start telling yourself things like *I am so full of joy, I am so loving, I am peaceful and calm,* or *I am wise with my finances.* Keep encouraging yourself in the things that you are now choosing to be. It may feel like a lie at first, but you will grow into it.

Perhaps you have been speaking negativity over your life, with thoughts like, *I'm so fat, broke, depressed,* etc. If those are seeds you have sewn and have been reaping the fruit, pull them out and start sewing new seeds now. Maybe those words took decades to sink in and have reaped plenty of fruit. Try clearing out the garden of your heart from this bad fruit and planting new seeds.

Don't give up encouraging yourself just because you don't see the fruit right away. When you have begun to plant new seeds in your own life, share the wealth, and start sowing seeds of good fruit into others' lives while you're at it. It will be like pouring Miracle Grow over both of your spirits and begin to change this world for the better, one person at a time.

Food for Thought

- What things have I been speaking over my life?
- How have I been speaking over the lives of others?
- How can I start speaking more beneficially to myself and others?

Selah.

Another Way

"Without counsel, purposes are disappointed; but in the multitude of counselors, they are established."

—Proverbs 15:22, KJV

I don't shy away from the fact that I used to be quite a moralist. I would like to say that it was only back when I believed I did everything perfectly. But if I'm honest, I find myself falling into the moralistic side of things simply because it seems much less messy than actually loving people and having grace.

I hope I have grown in this area, but before those years of growth, I was prideful, judgmental, and just not a nice person. I may have seemed nice on the outside, but on the inside, I was just another hurt person who hurt people. Even if it was just in my thoughts toward others, I'm sure it came across on the outside, even if I tried not to show it. On the outside, I thought I was the perfect Christian who went to church and led different ministries, but inside I was selfish, judgmental, and insecure.

Keeping Up and Remaining Human

I have seen this pressure so prevalent in Christian communities. Keeping up with the perceived life of the community around them becomes more important than seeking the sometimes messy and mysterious truths of God.

It's often so much harder to keep up with the Christians than it is with the Kardashians. After all, keeping up with the Kardashians just takes some money, a good plastic surgeon, and a subscription to the E! TV network. But keeping up with the Christians often requires feeling so guilty that you hide any past or current mistakes from anyone who may pass judgment, while worrying about committing any future sins that could be found out and shunned by the community. Depending on the Christian community, this might range from very public and permanent shunning to simply not returning calls or passive-aggressively ignoring the offender. But disapproving of a person because of their behavior doesn't leave much room for grace.

After all, how can anyone disapprove of a human created in God's image? Surely, we can have wrong behaviors, especially those behaviors that cause harm to ourselves and others. But the Bible makes it pretty clear that God disdains and considers the less public sins of greed, pride, superiority, and a calloused heart more harmful to the world than any sins of weakness.

In his book *The Immortal Diamond*, Richard Rohr writes about how Jesus constantly speaks against the sins of the spirit, the ego, and the false self much less than he does about the sins of the body. He goes on further to point out that Paul's deeper meaning for the word *flesh* is about our false outer self, not our body. So if God Himself says "the Word became flesh," our bodily flesh can't be bad. Otherwise, Christ would not have become flesh and God would not have made us this way, since He made humans by His own hand and declared us good.

I wonder how many other people are living in a way they know is not serving God, themselves, or anyone else, but just don't know how to get out of it? My encouragement to anyone who finds themselves in this place is to simply pray. Ask God to provide the way and to give you sight, strength, and courage to take it when it comes. Don't expect to be perfect. When we fall, we get up again just like Proverbs tells us. I challenge you to keep getting up again. Through prayer, wise counsel, and learning to hear God's voice, you can enter that alternative lifestyle of life more abundantly.

Food for Thought

- Have I been avoiding going to a church because of feeling inadequate to be there?
- Is there a way to connect with a community of faith that accepts me as I am now?
- How can my communities help foster acceptance? What can I do to help it happen?
- How can I pray this for my own faith community and for the church at large?

Selah.

106

Learn to Savor

"Don't copy the behavior and customs of this world, but let
God transform you into a new person by changing the way
you think. Then you will learn to know God's will for you,
which is good and pleasing and perfect."

—Romans 12:2, NLT

When I was a fitness instructor, I used to recommend eating everything
with chopsticks so that my clients would slow down, savor their food,
and become more aware of when they actually felt full. "How do I eat
cake and ice cream with chopsticks?" some clients would playfully
respond. I'd reply with a wry smile, "If you can't eat it with chopsticks,
maybe you shouldn't be eating it." I'm not opposed to cake or ice
cream, just to shoveling them into our mouths so fast that we hardly
notice when we've eaten three helpings and still want more.

Slow Down

The inability to slow down and develop awareness can lead to some
major problems. Even for people who are naturally thin, which seems
to be the socially desirable body type in a world of excess, their health
will still suffer if they continually make poor choices about what things
they choose to fuel their bodies. All kinds of maladies ranging from
heart disease, food allergies, autoimmune problems, obesity, diabetes,
and even cancer indicate that it is important to examine how we fill
our bodies.

Even so, what a greater importance it is to examine how we fill
the soul, since it is the eternal part of us, the part of us that feels and
experiences, connects, enjoys, and lives on forever.

Science is continually showing us that we cannot separate the
body from the spirit or the mind. They are all interconnected. We can
fill our bodies with the most organic healthy foods money can buy, but
if we are living stressed-out lifestyles, our bodies will not use those
nutrients to their full potential and disease will creep in anyway.

Enjoy What You Have

I have heard Americans say, "Oh, it hurts so good!" after consuming massive amounts of unhealthy food, particularly at holidays or social events. What they fail to realize is that it is not only their stomach that will hurt, but their whole body when this behavior is repeated over and over again. Not to mention that their emotional state will be altered by the chemicals being released to the brain and disrupting their natural ability to know when they are hungry or full.

It is so important to slow down and savor our food not only so we truly enjoy and taste it, but also to give our bodies a peaceful environment to digest. Some studies have shown that blessing a meal actually changes the chemical breakdown of the food eaten, others suggest this could be due to the act of stopping and breathing that allows the stomach to digest the food more thoroughly. Either way, stopping to be grateful for what we have can only benefit us.

The French expression *l'estomac n'a pas de dents* (translation, *the stomach does not have teeth*) is both a literal reminder to chew each bite to a liquid so that the stomach does not have to work so hard at digesting and a metaphoric reminder to breathe and slow the mind and body enough to savor and enjoy the food. Perhaps a soul equivalent would be *the soul does not have a liver.* We must make good choices for our souls and examine how we fill them. Are we taxing the liver of our souls by being workaholics, alcoholics, shopaholics, sex addicts, or worrywarts? Are we taking on any addictive behaviors that can be good in the proper context but become toxic to our spirits from abuse and overuse that leads us down the path of unfulfillment, anxious or depressed thoughts, and a general sense of apathy for our lives?

When Less is More

In my own life, I have struggled with being a love-aholic, so to speak. I needed constant reassurance that I was loved, valued, cared for, and good enough for whoever I was with. Yet, regardless of how much they reassured me, it was never enough. I had to learn not only to remember my true worth is in God, but also to savor the affirmations I was given. To hang onto them like beautiful love notes and reflect on those things when I was feeling the need for more, more, more.

The *bigger is better* mentality just isn't what it's cracked up to be. We see this in the obesity epidemic affecting much of the Western world. Bigger is not necessarily better. There comes a point when enough is just right. How do we train our brains to break away from the *bigger is better* mental programming into an *enough is perfect* mentality? Having a bit of overflow is great. But how do we break from our addictive behaviors long enough to just be grateful and realize we are enough, we have enough, and probably even have a bit more than we realized?

A whole host of things can be done to become the people we desire to be and no longer give into our old self-sabotaging habits. In his book *Breaking the Habit of Being Yourself,* Dr. Joe Dispenza says we can change these old patterns of behavior by consciously rewiring the neurons in our brains. Dr. Dispenza explains that neurons that no longer fire together no longer wire together, which means that when we become so aware of our old patterns we can consciously, and sometimes even verbally tell ourselves to change. With this consciousness and commitment to changing the patterns of our thinking, we actually change the genetic expression of our neurons.

The Bible would refer to this as "being transformed by the renewing of your mind," which can be done by prayer, intention, and commitment to change. Dr. Dispenza's book teaches principals for envisioning the new creation you desire to become and rehearsing being that person just as a musician rehearses for an upcoming performance. Science shows that by practicing firing neurons in a different way, we cause our genetics to express differently. In time, this genetic expression changes our inner world, which affects our outer world and leads us to live the lives we desire. Eventually, we can control our habits rather than allowing our habits to control us.

With this new way of thinking, we shift the mentality that we just can't help the people we are into a liberating notion that we are co-creators with God who have control over the expressions of our neuro-pathways and personal outcomes. Stopping, savoring, and developing awareness can literally change the direction of our lives.

Food for Thought

- What addictive or unconscious behaviors do I tend to repeat in my life?

- How do those behaviors affect my life experience?

- What is an area of my life that I would like to improve, and how could I rehearse being that future improved self?

- How does this person I choose to become think? Speak? Breathe? How would I treat myself and others?

- How can I meditate on this, allowing my neurons to change and my destiny to follow?

Selah.

The Gift of the Present

"Do not worry then, saying, 'What will we eat?' or 'What will we drink?' or 'What will we wear for clothing?' For the Gentiles eagerly seek all these things; for your heavenly Father knows that you need all these things. But seek first His kingdom and His righteousness, and all these things will be added to you."

—Matthew 6:31–33, NASB

I think about how so many people are incapable of savoring and enjoying the flavors of food. How can we come to an end of a meal and hardly remember the taste of what we have just eaten? When it's over, we barely paid attention to it, simply shoving it in our mouths.

How often do we do the same thing in our experience of life? So busy making sure all the details are perfect or just getting through it, that an entire season of life can pass by and we barely know it's over before it's gone.

Immersed in the Moment

When I hear parents reminisce about where the time has gone, I think of the story in the book of Luke when Jesus chides Martha for being anxious and troubled about so many things. Martha is running around the kitchen, trying to make all the preparations perfect for Jesus, then snaps at Jesus to tell her sister Mary to help her. Meanwhile, Mary had been so immersed in the moment, sitting at Jesus' feet and soaking up every word He had to say. Jesus basically tells Martha that she is so uptight and worried about all of these momentary things, but Mary is doing the one thing that is needed, the thing that will nourish her soul for all time.

I think about how many times Jesus speaks about people being worried about all of "these things." He says that we should seek first the kingdom, and "all of these things" will be added to us—food, clothing, shelter, [insert your worry here]. When we seek first being in the presence of God in His kingdom, He takes care of all of the tangible things; they all fall into place. When we are in God's presence, we don't have to worry about how we will work this or that thing out on our own, He takes care of us.

I think of how concerned Martha was about feeding Jesus, probably putting on the best spread she could possibly prepare. Little did she know that only a little while later, Jesus would feed thousands of people from a tiny boy's lunch with such overflow that there would be baskets of leftovers.

Jesus did not need what Martha had to give; she needed what He had to give, and the thing she was worried about (in this case, the food) would come one way or another.

The Flavor of Heaven

Think of the times that you have been so immersed in something you were enjoying, experiencing such focus that you completely forgot about eating. That is the way Christ desires us to savor life. The moments when we are completely engaged in each relationship or creative expression, learning about and loving people and enjoying moments together, are the times when we experience the heaven on earth that God created us for.

Savor moments alone with God, times together with friends; savor every flavor that this beautiful life has to offer. Resist the temptation to simply power through life, getting all the things done on your worry list. Instead, pray and enter the kingdom, rest in His flow and know that by being in God, all those things you once worried about will be taken care of, whether He uses you, someone else, or a miracle to do it.

Food for Thought

- What are the momentary things that cause me to worry most?
- How has God provided in the past?
- Would adopting an attitude of gratitude help me to focus on what I have rather than on what I feel I am lacking?
- Would spending moments savoring God and life and prayer perhaps lead to more effective solutions to my worries?

Selah.

Part 5:
Get to the Gym

A Washington Post article famously noted that gyms with the capacity to hold only three hundred people will enroll upwards of six thousand members. How do they keep from going out of business? Because they know most people sign up with every good intention but will never actually use their membership. This is why some wise gym-goers hire personal trainers or go to the gym with friends to keep their fitness goals on track.

It's no secret that life is lived more successfully together, which is where spiritual accountability comes in. Whether you find this through a friend, mentor, or coach, make sure to have proper support to help navigate questions, doubts, and those times when a healthy new habit seems like too much effort to keep up. A healthy spiritual life consists of much more than simply habits alone, which is why it is of utmost importance to seek wise counselors, spend time in quiet with your prayers and thoughts, and surround yourself with people who inspire you to enter more deeply into a richly satisfying (*more abundant*) spiritual life.

Spiritual Training

"Two are better than one, because they have a good return
for their labor; if either of them falls down, one can help the
other up. But pity anyone who falls and has no one to lift
them up."

—Ecclesiastes 4:10

When I was a Pilates instructor, I used to think to myself, *Is this really as effective as I say it is, or am I just so good at marketing that I have even convinced myself of its effectiveness as a means of job security?* Without fail, however, my clients would come in week after week with new testimonies about

113

how their backs were no longer stiff, how they could touch their toes for the first time in their lives, or how they could laugh and sneeze without fear of accidents. This constant flow of life-changing testimonies kept me in the fitness industry for over a decade.

Doubting Thomas to True Believer

The same thing happens in the spiritual world. I have been a doubting Thomas in my journey with God, wondering from time to time if this whole thing is only a made up story to control the masses and make people feel better about the inevitability of death or as real as I know it to be in my soul during those moments of heaven on earth where I have known God's closeness.

However, when I see changes not only in my own life, but hear testimonies of people's lives before they came to know the true peace that lies in the teaching of Christ, the journey it took them on, and the kinds of people they have become in the process, I can believe with a level of certain joy that these teachings aren't just some made-up fantasy to make us feel better about ourselves but a path to a true relationship with a living God who transforms our lives into something far more meaningful than we could imagine.

Though this meaningful life may be far from what culture markets as satisfying, we can truly enter into a peace that surpasses all understanding. There will inevitably be times of struggle and questioning throughout the process, as I have seen in myself and others when devoting time and energy to spiritual training. Our souls make a transformation far beyond the results of developing six-pack abs or touching one's toes for the first time, but of love and joy and truly touching hearts (perhaps also for the first time). Jesus becomes the Pilates instructor of our souls.

Transformation Before Proclamation

Please do not mistake my meaning here. I am not by any means suggesting that everyone claiming to be a Christian is transformed. Having a membership at a certain gym does not make a person fit, and neither does proclaiming membership to a certain brand of religion make a person holy. However, those who take advantage of this heavenly gym membership and seek the truth of spiritual training will certainly be changed in a way that impacts themselves and the lives around them in the most beautiful ways.

Christianity has received a bad rap in many parts of the world as the spiritual equivalent of an out-of-shape neighbor who tries to recruit others to participate in the newest fad diet with them. In a similar fashion, Christians are often viewed as trying to convert people to a brand of spirituality that hasn't appeared to transform them. This is not the Christianity that Jesus came to show the world, teaching us how to live free from the burdens of this world and the hierarchies built by its societies.

If being Christian means to be like Christ, then it's quite shocking that so many people claim the title without attempting to become anything like its namesake—who proclaimed that whoever truly listens to Him would see life-altering transformations in themselves and the world around them.

Of course, my fitness clients' bodies did not suddenly change, and their pain did not instantly go away. However, they may have noticed at some point that areas we had been working to change for months suddenly started feeling great after stretching, strengthening, and bringing balance to areas of misalignment.

The same is true in the Spirit. The decision to allow Christ to be your life trainer is not some get-fit-quick scheme, but a lifelong lifestyle change.

If we let God be our spiritual trainer, the decision takes only a moment, yet the process will be ongoing for the rest of one's life. It'll slowly change you until you hardly recognize what you looked like before. You will see a new creation who more closely each day resembles the divinity of the original design you were created for, just as Christ taught by example in the way He lived freely and confidently in His status as a child of God.

Food for Thought

- What aches in my soul could I bring to the Divine Trainer?
- What areas of weakness or stubbornness could I bring to God to be made strong or flexible?
- How could I become a more aware, obedient, trusting student?

Selah.

Stretch Your Soul

"You have changed my sadness into a joyful dance; you have taken away my sorrow and surrounded me with joy."

—Psalm 30:11

Eyes closed in deep satisfaction, I relished the aroma of fresh-burning incense floating from the front of the sanctuary and wafting toward to pews where I sat. Back straight, hands on my lap in an open posture of surrender and silent prayer, I began to relax. Sliding my large coat over my shoulders, I lifted my eyes to the high-domed ceilings above me and felt as if I were inside a giant Faberge egg. The choir hummed somewhere in the distance, where I could faintly hear their voices coalescing in some far-off hallway, and I felt myself exhale. Had I been holding my breath? "Hallelujah" they sang, "hallelujah." *The echo of my heart, the song of my soul.* My spirit lifted in a mutual *Hallelujah! Hallelujah to the King of Kings.* My breath caught, and I felt my nose prickle with unshed tears of gratitude for the present moment.

Notre Dame was stunning at night. The stained-glass windows were but shadows above the backlit arches of the hallways. The shinning lights spilled over every line and curve of the gothic-style cathedral, making its architecture stand out in a way that I had never noticed in the daylight. The illumination of the domed ceilings caused hues of golden light to radiate from their centers, the light fading into deep copper tones until it finally turned to black inside high-pointed arches where the stained-glass windows stole the scene by day, yet faded into the black background by night. The vision in front of me

116

was so magnificent that it hardly seemed real. It was like a set from a movie painted before my eyes.

It was in that moment that I heard a shuffling beside me and turned to see an old lady slowly and painfully walking down the aisle to my right. As she hobbled by, hunched and slightly dragging one outward-turned foot behind her, my heart sank in heaviness for her obvious pain.

Having been a Pilates instructor for nearly a decade, I frequently see people with postural problems that clearly cause a great deal of pain and think to myself, *I know how to fix that. If I could only have a few months of their lives and teach them private reformer classes a few days a week, the problems that have been worsening and ailing them all these years would be well on their way to healing, and their lives would drastically improve.* But private Pilates isn't cheap and takes a sacrifice of time and money that many won't make, even when it would equate to a life improvement that would far outweigh the cost.

I began mentally assessing the lady's posture and how it could be helped. Strengthen the right adductor to help turn the foot back in from the hip, stretch the pectoral muscles, and strengthen the rhomboids to pull her shoulders back, and work the erector spinal muscles to lift her back into an upright and considerably less painful position.

The deep hum of the church organ echoed through the great hall of the cathedral and shook me from my musing. A voice like a bell rang through the sanctuary and began to sing in the most beautiful French I had ever heard. "*Dieu, viens à mon aide! Seigneur, à notre secours!*" ("God, come to my aid! Lord, help us!") The angelic voices sang on and voices from pews all around me joined in mellifluous chorus.

Help us Lord, I thought, as the lyrics to the song planted themselves in my soul. *How many of us are walking with spiritual postures that cause us pain, yet we neglect to come to You for healing? How many of us are unwilling to follow You because we think the price is too costly? Yet You know more than we could ever understand how great the life improvement will be when You train our souls in Your perfect methods, when our heads are lifted by Your hand and our lives are lived in the abundance that we were created for.*

So many of us will never know. Like that poor lady, we will walk through life spiritually hobbled and hunched, never knowing that there is a way to walk upright again, that our mourning could be exchanged for dancing and our sorrows for joy.

Food for Thought:

- In what ways have I been spiritually hobbled or limping?
- Do I believe in God's healing for what ails me?
- What spiritual training might open my eyes to this healing?
- What might my prayer be for moving toward spiritual wholeness?

Selah.

Exercise for Your Soul

"Let them praise his name with dancing, making melody to Him with the tambourine and the lyre!"

—Psalm 149:3, ESV

In 2 Samuel 6, the Bible tells the story of King David quite literally dancing his shirt off in his celebration to the Lord, and we see how God delights in the expression of His people. One can only imagine the lively procession as Israel rejoiced with instruments, singing, and dancing while they brought the ark of the Lord and His blessing into their kingdom.

The interesting thing about this story is that, although all of Israel was celebrating in earnest, David's very own wife was looking on at him in disgust because she thought he was making a fool of himself...and in his undershirt no less! David's joyful self-expression comes in sharp contrast to his wife's—who, with all her propriety and piety, scolds him when he gets home...too uptight and worried about others' opinions to enjoy the moment. The story goes on to give a bleak glimpse into her passionless life, noting that she remained childless to the day of her death, which was about the worst thing that could happen to a woman of her time.

Express Your Soul

In relation to the soul, self-expression is my exercise. It's a lot like any other skill and a lot like muscle. If you don't use it, you lose it—but you can always practice again and get it back.

Stifle your self-expression, however, and your soul will become lethargic and apathetic. When we express our true selves, allowing the life within us to flow out in rivers of overflowing life, we glorify the One who breathed that life into us.

When was the last time you danced just for the fun of it? The last time you spent time writing, drawing, painting, sculpting, doing photography, or whatever else it is that makes your soul feel free and allows your imagination to run wild in a field of dreams and inspiration?

So many of us lose this self-expressive part of ourselves as we grow up in a world of number-crunching, fact-learning, and money-making madness. We forget how to dream, create, write, paint, draw, dance, sing, color... do whatever it was we once did to give our rational minds a break from the linear, black-and-white world it functions in day to day. Think about the colors that may be added to your life as you make space for the creative, allow room for the fanciful, and dance like nobody is watching.

Food for Thought

- What creative pastimes did I enjoy as a child? Singing? Coloring? Guessing the shapes of clouds?
- How could giving my mind space to imagine and create benefit other areas of my life and add an element of peace to my spirit?
- When can I make time to creatively express myself? What will I do?

Selah.

Find Your Community

"In essentials, unity; in nonessentials, liberty; in all things, love."

—St. Augustine of Hippo

When I was young, my family moved to Borneo. *Literally*. We lived one house away from pure jungle, which welcomed large-fanged primates to jump into our yard to eat from our banana tree, cobras to slither around our gutters, alligators to rummage through our garbage cans, geckos to scramble up the walls inside and outside the house—and we lived pretty well.

My father was a pilot for the Sultan of Brunei, who was the wealthiest man in the world at the time, which blessed us with a home in one of the more developed areas of the country. This early childhood experience gave me the privilege of attending international school in Brunei alongside kids from more countries around the world than I could count. The most amazing thing about growing up this way was that everyone was different, which made everyone pretty much the same in a very beautiful way.

We all lived in a unity with so many different cultures, styles, and personalities—accepted just as we were. Nobody made fun of me for my dated American style; or the Indian kids for their more traditional wear; and certainly not the nation's eight-year-old princesses for the elegant gowns, large petty coats, and golden treasure chests around their necks each day at school. This became a beautiful phase of life that I definitely took for granted as normal. It was how I thought the world worked before I moved back to America.

In America, the kids all wore the same brands of clothing, walked in the same sneakers, listened to the same music, and watched the same television programs. And watch out if you didn't do it too! I can remember being teased for dressing in a different clothing style, having no clue who the New Kids on the Block were, and never watching television in the several years spent I spent in a third-world country.

American culture shock was far worse than anything I had experienced moving to Borneo as a kid. I quickly learned that somewhere ingrained in American culture is an inability to appreciate differences. Not only did people here *not* appreciate differences, but I would get chastised for them. As I continued to grow up along the Southwest coast of the United States, I saw families choose not to teach their children their native languages so that they could more easily blend in to mainstream society, and I was completely baffled. Why in the world did American culture need to be one-size-fits-all?

Then I began to study business. The most successful companies were the ones that studied the trends, appreciated and followed them where necessary, but ultimately broke the mold. The next big thing would come from those who could think outside of the cultural box that the masses so eagerly squeezed themselves into. I decided this was the kind of person I wanted be—regardless of which country I was in.

Fitting into the Church Mold

Now that I travel for a living and participated in different churches around the world, I've experienced a spectrum of different church cultures. There are churches where everyone must think the same, dress the same, and *for goodness' sake,* they must believe the exact same interpretation of scripture. In these churches, individual search for truth in God is often stifled by strict adherence to the particular church's statements of belief. It reminds me of the stifling feelings of self-expression I felt coming back to America after my adventures in Borneo. And I can't help noticing that the church communities that are true to themselves, their members, and their faith are always the most welcoming—where all walks of life, viewpoints, and seasons of faith are valued and celebrated.

If churches were equivalent to gyms in our fitness analogy, then it would seem to make sense that most people would enjoy a big box gym with locations everywhere. But Jesus said anywhere that two or three people are gathered is essentially church. Maybe your soul's best exercise community will be in a small mom and pop shop with a devoted group of others dedicated to encouraging you to keep attending; maybe it'll be in private sessions with a close friend or two. Perhaps Christians can stop putting God in a box of what we think church and Christianity should look like and focus on becoming our truer selves through the lens of Christ and His teachings. He taught that people would know who we are by the way we love one another, so let's love one another and let the details take care of themselves.

Food for Thought

- What feels like the most authentic form of church for me?
- Can I think of someone I admire who enjoys a completely different approach to community with God?
- How can I bring unity and love to the communities I belong to?

Selah.

For the Love of God

"I appeal to you, brothers and sisters, in the name of our Lord Jesus Christ, that all of you agree with one another in what you say and there be no divisions among you, but that you be perfectly united in mind and thought."

—1 Corinthians 1:10

I spent one summer attending a European country church filled with love and connection to God. The church community consisted of mostly Americans with a few Europeans who attended many events together, and I enjoyed participating in many of their children's programs, worship teams, and getting to know the people. You could imagine my surprise when I received a troubling message from one of its members. The message detailed how lovely it was to meet me; however, the person was very concerned that I posted messages from pastors whom they believed to be heretical false prophets. The message concluded with their hope that the Lord would guide me into the *narrow* path of Christ.

I was livid. Not because this person was accusing me of believing false prophets, but because of the people I have seen hurt by similar accusations in churches before. Someone whose knowledge of the Bible was less extensive or whose faith was still new may be completely swayed or even turned away from church altogether because of a message like this. One person's judgmental opinion about a pastor whom they have likely never listened to for themselves could sway new believers to question their faith, wonder if they were really Christians, worry if they had gotten the whole thing wrong, or even worse—start accusing other people who listen to those particular Bible teachers as listening to false prophets simply because they'd been told the same.

I could think of several people who could assume they were definitely not on this *narrow* path, that God certainly did not wish to see *all* His creation saved, and therefore might give up on seeking Jesus altogether, missing out on the kind of life they could have enjoyed by growing in a deeper relationship with Him that comes with years of learning His ways and walking in the wisdom the various pastors teach.

Narrow Path or Narrow Mind?

This message came with no reasons for why the person believed these particular preachers were heretics or false prophets and absolutely no scriptural basis for why this person felt the way they did about them. Upon much reflection, a bit of calming down, and a lot of prayer, I wrote my best response explaining why I appreciated their concern but disagreed with their judgment. Their reply was radio silence, but that's okay.

The thing I had to remember was that this person truly thought that they were being helpful and warning me about what they believed were false teachings. This is why it's so important to be familiar with biblical texts, read the Bible ourselves, and seek truth in prayer and contemplation. Regurgitating whatever information any pastor or spiritual person tells us is not a way to develop our own true faith or more fully become our true selves.

I also tend to be wary of any individual or teacher who points fingers at other individuals or teachers about their faith and the way it is expressed. Abraham Lincoln wisely said, "a house divided against itself cannot stand," and a few millennia prior to that, Jesus said a very similar statement in Matthew 12. Living in peace and love with one another does not mean we must agree on everything, but rather live in peace and unity in all things.

As with any pastors, we must be aware of personal biases and make sure to read the Bible for ourselves. Jesus says that we will know false prophets by their fruit and that bad trees cannot produce good fruit. As Christians, we may have differing opinions about what makes a good pastor or biblical teacher—maybe you think someone doesn't get very deep or focuses too specifically on certain topics—yet I have found, in my nearly 25 years of faith in Christ and studying under a multitude of Bible teachers from various backgrounds, that it is important to consider avoiding fighting over the nonessentials and focus on love instead.

Love Conquers Division

What did Jesus say were the essentials? I've already noted Jesus' cut and dry explanation in Matthew 22 to love God and others and let everything else work itself out. All of the other theological laws and commandments depend first on a loving heart.

Paul says a similar thing in 1 Corinthians when he explains that, without love, none of the other elements of faith (like prophecy or miracles) mattered. Without a heart and spirit full of love, none of this Christianity stuff really matters. This lack of love for one another has turned away so many people who were once seeking the love and truth that Christ came to give. In the same chapter, Paul outlines what true love actually looks like: patient, kind, humble, polite, and not insisting on its own way.

How many different denominations are pointing fingers at one another and insisting on their own way? I wonder if Christ's response to them would have been the same. Of all the theological points made by one denomination or another, might Jesus simply tell us that all our points mean nothing if we refuse to truly love God and each other?

Food for Thought

- In what ways do I seek truth for myself?
- Have I accused others of believing incorrectly? Why have I done this?
- What have I thought of as the essentials of a good faith, and how does that compare to what Christ taught?

Selah.

One-Point Jesus-ist

"Call to Me and I will answer you, and I will tell you great and mighty things, which you do not know."

—Jeremiah 33:3

I once watched a sermon with a friend about five-point Calvinism. The preacher was very thorough about the history of John Calvin, how it came about, why he believed the way he did, and what the five points of Calvin's belief system were based on. This pastor, however, only believed in 4.5 of the points and explained that he was a 4.5-point Calvinist.

At the end of the sermon, I turned to my friend and said, "Well, I am a one-point Jesus-ist."

All those points are fine and make sense, but I believe the essential thing Jesus focused on was to love God and love each other. With faith in Christ and study of the scripture, the rest will fall into place in different ways at different times for different people.

Finding God in the Differences

Though there are many denominations and people seeking Christ in ways that may look different, there is no need to point fingers at the way others believe in Jesus. We're all seeking the same thing. Jesus said that those who seek will find Him. He goes on to say that if human parents do not give their children things that are harmful when they ask for something helpful, how much more will God give helpful things to people who seek Him?

Seeking God with all our hearts and holding on to all His promises will help us to truly find what we are seeking. This path will certainly look different for different people because God made us all different. So why should we expect our faith to look exactly the same? As we seek God, love Him and His Son with all of our hearts, and love the people He created (including ourselves and those vastly different from us), we focus on the essentials in which every believer can have unity. The nonessentials of different interpretations of what faith should look like can be met with liberty, and all things met with charity, good will, and love.

Even as a very mature believer, I think it is important to know that we do not have *the* definitive answer to every theological question. A very wise person once told me, "There is ultimate truth, but none of us have it." That same teacher taught me that the Bible is just as mysterious as Christ Himself was when He walked the earth. So, we must allow the mysteries to be revealed when ours hearts are ready and be okay with some mysteries remaining that way.

Food for Thought

- What outward things have I considered make me a person of faith?
- Do those things come from a place of love for God and others?
- If they don't, do I believe God can transform my heart to become more loving?

Selah.

Ugly Duckling Grace

"Provide for those who grieve in Zion—to bestow on them a
crown of beauty instead of ashes, the oil of joy instead of
mourning, and a garment of praise instead of a spirit of
despair. They will be called oaks of righteousness, a
planting of the Lord for the display of his splendor."

—Isaiah 61:3, NIV

In the story of the prodigal son, in Luke 15, Jesus talks about a son who squanders away all of his inheritance on "wild living"—while his father is alive, no less. When he finds himself in dirt longing to eat the slop that pigs are eating, he finally realizes that perhaps he should go home and apologize.

But this wasn't a modern Western society where parents were expected to accept their children regardless of how they choose to live their lives; this was a society of honor where this son had just dishonored his father to the point of essentially saying, "I can't wait for you to die; just give me your money now." It was the kind of action that would cause sons of that day to be completely disowned, forever.

When the father welcomed him home as if he had just come back to life, the son in this story would have known what kind of a social sacrifice that would take for his father. Though we do not see his appreciation displayed in the story, we do see the bitterness of the older brother who stuck around, felt that he had done everything right, and didn't want his brother to be welcomed back home. It isn't a pretty sight.

Safe Spaces

People who say they have never questioned God in any capacity make me wonder how that could be possible. How can we have grace and compassion for fallen, broken, totally screwed up people if we have never been there ourselves? Many of us moralistic Christians probably relate most to the older brother in that story, thinking we do everything perfectly and those who can't get their act together should not be accepted by God, much less anyone else. Too often, we *older brother* types are quick to look down our noses at other Christians' imperfections, thinking anyone who isn't a *good Christian* is just a heathen obviously not worthy of the narrow, pious path.

Have you ever met someone who is kind, good looking, and way too nice to have been that way all of their life? Then you find out they were the ugly duckling who was never cool or popular growing up, and it all seems to make sense. They know what it is like to be the one ridiculed and put down, so they make an extra effort to build up others and show the kindness they wish they had received when they were younger.

I see the same thing in many people who call themselves Christians. The people who have fallen away or *gone prodigal* at some point, who made some big mistakes and come back to Christ seem to be the kindest, most compassionate ones who others come to when they need grace. They are the ones who people will confess to because they have been there and can meet someone in their low points without judgment. One thing we must realize is that we have all sinned and fallen short of the glory of God, which means we can show grace to ourselves and every other human who has fallen too.

Beauty in the Cracks

When you've walked where another has walked, you will not belittle the person who is earnestly seeking to live better. You will meet them with compassion, as Jesus did for the woman caught in adultery. He did not condemn her. When those of us who haven't lived perfect lives—who've perhaps made bigger mistakes for longer periods of time than we would like to admit—can receive compassion from loving Christians when confessing our sins, we're able to live more like Jesus than the older brother and judgmental Pharisees who are depicted negatively throughout stories in the Bible.

This may sound heretical, and perhaps it is, but I think it's good for a Christian to fall away and come back to their faith at some point after becoming a Christian. Perhaps this is part of what it means that we must lose our lives in order to find them. If God is the potter and I am the clay, then I know that I have been broken many times. Fallen again and again, perhaps with cracks from each fall, with patches of different materials where the fragments are too broken to put back—but this is the eclectic mosaic of beauty God continues to make and form me in. He makes us all into new creations when we bring our lives humbly before Him. Not all at once, but little by little, fall after fall, lesson after lesson, He gives us beauty for ashes.

Food for Thought

- Do I identify more with the prodigal son or older brother in this story?
- In what areas do I judge others who might benefit from a more gracious response?
- In what areas have I fallen that I can bring to God and seek more personal grace?
- Can I think of a time where I have brought the broken pieces of my life to God and He has given me beauty for those ashes? How has He made me into more than I was before?

Selah.

Part 6:
Training Is Everything

Durham University, an English public research institution, associates the benefits of receiving impartial advice and encouragement from a coach or mentor with developing supportive relationships, assistance with problem solving, improved self-confidence, professional growth, and ability to reflect on one's practice. Likewise, the Bible also promotes the benefit of having a "multitude of wise counselors" and outright says that spending time with wise people helps you become wise, too.

Having many mentors, therapists, and coaches over my own lifetime, I have seen how having a wise outside perspective into my life has both helped me see my own blind spots and encouraged me to grow and mature in ways that relying only on peer-based relationships could not. It is because of these coaches and mentors that I have been able to grow more deeply in my faith and my connection with humanity and find more peace than I could have ever imagined in my early life.

Meditating Day and Night

"Blessed is the one who does not walk in step with the
wicked or stand in the way that sinners take or sit in the
company of mockers, but whose delight is in the law of
the LORD, and who meditates on His law day and night. That
person is like a tree planted by streams of water, which yields
its fruit in season and whose leaf does not wither—whatever
they do prospers."

—Psalm 1:2–3, NIV

Yoga brought me back to God. Through this form of moving meditation, I learned how to listen to my body and my spirit. In my

131

yoga practice, I began to notice when my body was stressed or when my body and mind were in balance. When I was unable to balance in certain poses, it often originated from an imbalance in an area of my inner life. Developing this awareness gave me the ability to find the imbalances in my life and take action toward changing them. I began to get to know and understand myself in a completely new, more intimate way…and I missed God.

Finding the Way Home

Having walked away from church years before, imagine my surprise, when I began to realize that feeling a lack of spirituality left me I feeling a major imbalance in my life. Yoga can be a controversial subject in some conservative Christian circles, but it has been a big part of the path that led me personally closer to Christ. I am incredibly grateful for the stillness, allowance, and flow I have learned through yoga practice.

Soon, I was seeking out God again and looking for a church to attend. I was very unsure what or if I believed about organized religion at that point, so I approached finding a church cautiously—walking out of one local church service after another as soon as they said anything that I found mildly offensive, believing that the whole church thing simply wasn't for me anymore.

When I decided to attend the contemplative prayer discussions, I started to learn more about this way of living in community that did not focus on judging how moral the people were. As I spent more time in a group of Christians who focused instead on seeking Jesus in silence and discussion and on showing each other kindness without judgment, my inner and outer life began to move into greater balance. This was a graceful love of Christ, and it was different from the rigid, rule-following way I had thought of God in the past.

My life did not change overnight, and I was still living in a way that would probably shock and appall many Christians. But Christ met me where I was, in a very real way that I could accept and understand but not explain. This new awareness of Jesus drawing me near to His Spirit did not change my morals or actions immediately, but it did draw me in with curiosity and desire to know the truth of God more fully. This curiosity ultimately led me to a path that would heal me, make me whole, and lead me into a life more abundant than I could have possibly hoped for or imagined at the time.

Soul-Stirring Stillness

I realize more and more each day that God continues to stir curiosity in me each moment of my life and will continue to do so until I see Him face to face. Until that day comes, I desire to seek Him in the silence, to wait on Him in the stillness, and to meditate on His Word day and night.

What a wonder it is to meditate and be still enough to see that everything in nature is moved by God. His hand moves the waves in the sea and leaves on the trees. When we become still enough to let Him, His very breath can also move our hearts and souls. Though it's not always a perfect acceptance, this stillness in my soul helps me allow Him to move me so that I may flow in the goodness of His love and surrender to the sacred rhythm of life He is continuously breathing into me.

Food for Thought

- What does meditation mean to me?
- How could listening for God's still, small voice affect my prayer life?
- What can I become aware of within and around me that God is continuously breathing into?

Selah.

Wisdom Sets the Course

"Do not forsake wisdom, and she will protect you; love her,
and she will watch over you."

—Proverbs 4:6

Every year, I travel to Russia with an organization that teaches wisdom and life skills to orphans who have recently aged out of their orphanages with no experience how to interact in the working world, manage living expenses, or care for themselves for the first time.

Over the last several years, I have taught a business and finance course on the basics of saving more and spending less. Ultimately, our primary goal is to impart to them wisdom that will carry them through decision-making, helping them to become diligent in all they do and live lives that will bring joy to God, themselves, and others.

Ask any class participants what phrase I repeat more than anything during these business classes, and anyone will tell you: "Read Proverbs." That may seem like strange advice for a business and finance class; however, I have read through Proverbs enough times to know that it contains all the principals one needs to succeed in life. The wisdom contained in this book gets richer and more profound every time you read it.

A Proverb a Day Keeps Folly Away

The biblical book of James says that all we have to do is ask God for wisdom, and He will freely give it to us without finding fault. To put it in action, look no further than the book of Proverbs—covering everything from who we spend time with and how we spend that time to how we speak, who we ask for counsel, how to be humble and honest, and so much more.

If you are new to the Bible, I highly recommend starting with a chapter of Proverbs a day. There are 31 chapters—one for every day of the month! I cannot count how many times I have read these verses, but I can say that they speak life and wisdom into my soul each time I do. Another great thing about the Proverbs is that they are short and a good way to start a habit that is not too cumbersome to make part of an ongoing routine. The lessons contained within this short book are no less profound the 100th time I read them than they were the first. On reflection, they not only teach wisdom, but give hope as well.

Psalms are great for this too, with poem after poem reminding us that there are times in life for all kinds of emotions and that God will use our joy and our suffering both for our good and His glory. The Psalms are also quite short and remind us that we can express our greatest joys and deepest agonies to our Creator because He cares.

Wisdom fills the pages of the entire Bible—full of stories of tragedy and triumph, love and loss, and poetry that speaks to hearts throughout the ages. For readers less familiar with scripture, it may be hard to understand and process whole chapters at once, yet for some it may be more interesting to read through entire stories. All to be learned from, felt, meditated on, and respected for their various forms of teaching.

Consider the Genre

As important as it is to read the Scriptures, it is just as important to respect each genre of scripture for what it is. When reading a section of scripture written as poetry meant to convey a feeling, pray for space to allow those feelings to move you in response to the living and feeling God who inspired them. Read historical accounts with a thirst for knowledge of facts and figures from that specific period in time.

In these stories of tragedy and loss, promises long fulfilled, and people constantly rebelling against a God who keeps chasing them to offer His love and claim them once again as His own, we can see our own folly. We can see how we have also been saved from our enemies in unexpected ways…even when those enemies have been our own pride, ego, and false selves.

In biblical stories like Esther's, we can find courage; in Ruth's, we find humility and grace. And in all, we can find God's goodness even when it is expressed through tragedy, loss, war, and failure. In the story of Joseph, we can see that the things others may have done to harm us actually ended up helping push us to a place of greater influence and blessing.

From the biblical stories of peoples' lives, pray you will learn by applying the wisdom to your own life without repeating the mistakes of the characters within. Pray it will inspire you to trust in God as you pursue the dreams He has placed on your own heart.

Regardless of where you choose to start reading scripture, take a few aspects into consideration: thoughtfully consider the genre and the audience that the passage was written for and prayerfully consider how the passage may relate to your own life today. I once heard a monk say that very little of the scripture is meant to be taken literally, but all is meant to evoke a feeling that leads to a change of heart, producing a more fully developed human.

Food for Thought

- When I read my Bible, do I take the different genres into consideration, or do I try to understand everything literally?
- How can the Scriptures come more alive for me?
- How could applying biblical wisdom to my life help me make decisions that enhance the purposes I have been created to live on this earth?

Selah.

Start Where You Are

"I have taught you the way of wisdom; I have led you in the paths of uprightness. When you walk, your step will not be hampered, and if you run, you will not stumble."

—Proverbs 4:11–12, ESV

I often think of the day I will have children of my own and can share wisdom with them, like Solomon shares with his son in this verse from Proverbs 4. I consider that, if I had a daughter, I'd rewrite every verse from "son" to "daughter," so she could feel its message more personally in her heart. Then, I contemplate other cultures that more highly value handed-down wisdom—where grandparents tell stories to teach their grandchildren and parents intentionally teach lessons of

136

wisdom to their children—where wisdom is sought after as precious treasure.

American culture as a whole tends to lack intentionality. Going through the motions and just getting through a life that inevitably feels so hard seems to be the norm for many modern Americans. Perhaps life *is* much harder because wisdom has never been passed down from one generation to another.

Walking Upright

When I read that verse, I think about how many people's steps have been hampered. How many have grown up without wise teaching or examples of how to walk wisely in this life, instead watching and modeling ways that lead to destruction. I do not mean the destruction of hell, and I don't think that's what the Bible meant either. I mean things that are painful for our souls here and now. Things like divorce, addiction, adultery, laziness, greed, anxiousness, and depression all keep us from living rich and full lives. We cannot even blame it on the generation before us, because many of them did not see wisdom exemplified to them either.

The same is true with all kinds of wisdom, ranging from financial advice to marital guidance. I've seen statistics show that people with divorced parents were much more likely to get a divorce themselves, and those whose parents remarried were even more likely to get divorced because it reinforced the mentality of disposable relationships in a disposable society.

If this is true, does it mean all hope is lost? Are children of divorce simply doomed to become statistics? Of course not! However, how much better could it be for the next generation if we, like Solomon in the above proverb, teach our children the ways of wisdom, both in actions and words, and lead them in paths of righteousness to help better guide their steps through life?

We must also give ourselves and others grace for the ways we did not have the advantage of experiencing wisdom and righteousness or perhaps were led in quite opposite detrimental directions altogether. Extend this grace to the generations before us who modeled the lack of wisdom that they themselves never learned, perpetuating the foolishness they saw in their own upbringing.

Over the years, I've beaten myself up over some things that I've looked to the generations before me in anger and thought, *If you had only dealt with this, it would not have taken me the better part of the last decade to overcome!* But we must all play with the cards we are dealt. Some people have financially astute, happily married parents, while others' parents may suffer from addiction, or still others may have no parents at all. We need to check our privilege in all ways—not just in relationships and finances, but in the emotional and spiritual aspects of life, as well.

Pride and Privilege

I am fascinated by YouTube videos of privilege walks. These usually take place in camp settings with students listing a series of statements ranging from *step back if your ancestors were forced to come to the United States without their choice* to *step forward if you have never skipped a meal out of necessity.* Students step forward and back based on statements that were completely out of their control to see where they end up on a scale of privilege. Then they're asked to race toward a finish line. Some start the race already at the finish line, while others are still at the beginning of the field. It would be heinous to judge the person from the back of the field of privilege for not making it to the finish line as quickly and easily as those right up front, yet that's what we often do in society and spirituality as well.

Perhaps this is part of what Jesus meant when He said the first will be last and the last will be first. That He does not judge us by where we are in the line of privilege or societal cast, but He sees our hearts, our focus, and how steadfastly we run toward the finish line. Yet, so many Christians judge their fellow believers' spiritual journeys based on their own privileged beginnings.

Many Christians who have known nothing but happy families and life "in the church" judge others who turn to behaviors that fulfill their cravings of belonging, comfort, and intimacy that they don't receive at home or in the church. Other Christians see their ego-driven false selves as pillars of sacrifice because they are able to resist

138

temptation better than the rest. Unfortunately, these are often the same people that fall the hardest and have a more difficult time returning to God because their faith is based on earning their way to salvation by the *good* things they do outweighing the *bad* things they are strong enough to resist.

When people who depend on their own strength realize that nobody is moralistically *good enough* (even themselves), finding pure grace in Christ can be a long journey. It can be a tough road to realizing it has absolutely nothing to do with who we think we are or how we want to be seen, but everything to do with who we were created to be. When we learn the wisdom that leads to grace with ourselves, we can share it with others and help change the world one graceful act at a time—becoming an example that affects generations to come.

Food for Thought

- Where would I consider myself on the field of spiritual privilege?
- Were wise or foolish decisions modeled in my upbringing?
- Have I succumb to or overcome the patterns of my upbringing?
- Am I loving and gracious in my thoughts about myself and others?

Selah.

Our Souls Crave Nutrition

"And let us consider how we may spur one another on toward love and good deeds, not giving up meeting together, as some are in the habit of doing, but encouraging one another—and all the more as you see the Day approaching."

—Hebrews 10:24–26 (NIV)

Have you ever really craved a certain food, only to find nothing remotely like it in your house? You rummage through the cupboards and eat a bunch of things that are not what you really want, then sit down with a bellyache and a craving still raging on?

Humans are created for intimacy—with God and each other. The further we separate from that, the more we corrupt the intended beauty for which we were created. Yet, the further we separate from this divinely inspired intimacy, the more we will crave it. This is often where abuse of beautiful things comes into the picture, where we see perversion of all kinds, because the soul will crave what it will crave and keep consuming until it finds it.

Sweet Intimacy

Several studies and articles suggest that the artificial sweeteners added to diet colas to eliminate the calories actually cause our bodies to crave more sweets, leading to further feelings of hunger, and ultimately excess weight gain. The modern Western diet is full of so many artificial sweeteners, and the modern Western spiritual diet is on a similar path.

Many of us are serving ourselves the diet soda equivalent for human intimacy. We settle for online relationships instead of interacting face to face, for shallow friendships instead of depth, for hooking up instead of commitment. All because we are afraid of the carbs associated with that commitment, with depending on someone and having them depend on us. We're afraid to commit to friendships, being there through the trials and the joys, and trusting one another to be supportive during those ups and downs. We're wary of staying committed to our families in the complexities that come with supporting each other when we know their past mistakes. Many of us settle for a shallow group of friends who never truly know us, leaving us feeling lonely in a crowd of people. It can be like drinking a 12-pack of diet soda when you could have had the natural fructose energy of a few fresh-pressed juices instead.

Fresh-pressed juices are more expensive, take longer to prepare and clean up, and cannot stay in their original condition sitting on the shelf forever; however, the nourishment they provide will be exponentially better than the soda—fulfilling, refreshing, and nourishing the cells of the body rather than destroying it and leading it to crave more of the wrong thing. Nurturing our relationship with God and with the people around us is like choosing the necessary expense, prep time, and cleanup to enjoy a fresh-pressed juice. It will cost more, but the abundance of added health and vitality will be immeasurably worth it.

Healthy Relationships, Happy Life

Nourishing foods are the staple of a healthy lifestyle. To consistently feed the brain and body, providing the carbohydrates, fats, and proteins they need to function at an optimal level is imperative. Anyone who has ever begun the journey to a healthier lifestyle knows that if you fail to plan, you plan to fail. When it comes to the body, it is important to make time for preparing and eating nourishing foods and keeping healthy snacks such as nuts on hand when on the go.

When it comes to the soul, we must make sure we are surrounding ourselves with people who desire a similar depth of right relationship as we do, that we are feeding our minds and our spirits the daily bread of God's words, and that we are taking time to speak our prayers and listen for the answers. All these things nourish the soul. Intimacy with God shows us how to engage in right relationship that leads to intimacy with the people around us.

In the book *The Seven Levels of Intimacy*, author Matthew Kelly notes that we will not have the same level of intimacy with a cashier who checks our groceries as we will with our closer relationships such as family, close friends, or spouses. When we seek to love God and others, the relationships we have, regardless of intimacy level, will naturally progress in a more loving and kind dimension. When we genuinely love someone, we pay attention to their needs and desires and do what we can to help them fulfill those needs and desires as best we can. As we learn to love the nourishment of true intimate relationships with people, we will never be able to settle for the artificially sweetened versions again.

Holy Hydration

When we live in intimate connection with God, intimate connection with others will flow much more naturally. We will have more to give because we are filled with what Jesus called living water.

Consider the woman at the well who had five husbands and was living unmarried to a sixth man—completely unacceptable for a woman of her time. Jesus tells her that He could give her living water, and she'd never thirst again. He basically told her that she was throwing her bucket down all the wrong wells because the enormity of love that she needed could only come from one source: His love. No one person's well is deep enough to quench the craving for intimacy with our Creator that our souls long for. Each time the woman approached a new relationship with the hopes of being fulfilled, she only left thirsty again. Jesus then came along and promised that whoever would drink the metaphoric water that His love gave would be so full that they would be like a spring welling up with love forever.

As a former love addict, I really relate to this woman. I craved every call, message, or morsel of time spent that I could get from every romantic relationship. I would be so excited that a person thought I was special that I would need more and more of the *water* they had to give. I would bleed their wells dry, then wonder why the relationship came to an end. Only by the grace of God was I able to recognize this pattern and remind myself to focus on Christ and His divine love within me, receiving my *living water*, value, and worth from within.

Is it any wonder that the three- or seven-year itch exists, that we often start to look outside our committed relationships for new excitement? After all, what happens when your skin gets really dry? It itches! God's divine hydration is the only thing that will ever fulfill the deep thirst for unconditional love that we all have.

Some of us have addictions that were formed before we were even old enough to recognize—cravings for love, affection, acceptance, and belonging. I read a quote by Dr. Jenn Mann that said, "It has been said that we can get an accurate picture of what we didn't get in our childhoods by looking at our chronic complaints about our relationships." This may be true, but the beautiful thing is that it is never too late to bring awareness to those deficiencies and change our minds and our lives toward craving the proper nutrients and hydration that never run dry.

Food for Thought

- In what ways do I crave intimacy?
- Would I consider my relationships healthy, deep, and life-giving?
- How could the *living water* of Christ's love bring new life into my relationships with God, myself, and others?

Selah.

Part 7:
Curbing Unhealthy Cravings

Creamy, cold ice cream melting on top of a freshly baked thick chocolate chip cookie—sounds good, right? Or maybe not. This mental picture either makes your mouth start watering or kind of grosses you out. If you're satiated with nourishing food that makes your body feel alive and vibrant, it probably doesn't sound so appealing.

When do our cravings tend to get the best of us? Is there wisdom in the axiom to never grocery shop on an empty stomach? We know that cravings can get the best of us when our self-restraint is at a low point. Creating strategies around avoiding temptations, like being well-nourished before going to the supermarket, will almost always lead to hitting our life goals just a bit closer to the target we are aiming for. So, how does this relate to spiritual health and strength?

What True Intimacy Really Looks Like

"It is our lonely and fearful illusion of separateness that makes us do sinful and selfish things."

—Richard Rohr

What is intimacy? Is it clothes-tearing, wild, uncontrollable lust for someone like movies and television portray it to be? Is it simply sex? Or is it something else? Perhaps something deeper? Is it all of that and also something deeper? Something not quite explainable? Have we been so inundated with exposure to what we are told intimacy should look like that we no longer know what the real thing is, let alone desire it?

Are we rapidly becoming like characters in Pixar's *Wall-E* movie, trying to plant a pizza tree because we no longer know what real spiritual fruits and vegetables look or taste like? Are we forgetting what is real in all areas of our lives? In a culture that wants microwave-fast results for food, relationships, careers, and satisfaction, is there room for savoring gourmet slow cooking anymore? Who really wants a meal cooked in a microwave when it's possible to have an artfully prepared meal from the oven and skillet?

The problem isn't that intimacy no longer exists but that we have forgotten how it looks and tastes. We have busied ourselves to the point of wanting convenience over quality. It is my prayer that all of humanity would make it our mission to rediscover the true treasures of life, the things that nourish the soul—the intimacy that leads to happiness, right relationships, and fulfillment beyond what we have ever known.

Boxing Ourselves In

Intimacy—or our lack thereof—seems to be a hot topic these days. In a *Thrive Global* article, writer Marina Rose explains that, although the use of technology and media has connected people more than ever before in human history, somehow, we are actually feeling increasingly more lonely.

Many of us so-called well-connected people tend to isolate ourselves, whether due to demanding jobs that keep us from our loved ones or simply because we're not setting aside the time to spend with the people who matter most to us. This revelation has caused me to give deep thought to how I spend my days and who I spend them with. In a world where being swamped with work or too busy to make a phone call is considered a badge of honor, I've paused to wonder if all this busyness is really a good thing.

A decade ago, the New York Times cautioned that loneliness leads to poorer physical and mental health, with the BBC years later declaring loneliness to be a "hidden killer of the elderly." Five years ago, CNN published findings that "tight-knit local communities may help to reinforce and encourage certain types of behaviors that protect against cardiovascular damage." But we still aren't listening.

It's hard to deny that social interaction and close relationships are essential for a healthy and balanced life. So, why is it that so few of us take the time to nurture our relationships and spend time with those we care about? Whatever drives us toward isolation, our culture seems to be lonelier than ever.

Much of modern society worships independence and seclusion, a progression that's accelerated in recent decades. In many parts of the country, we can drive straight into our garages, walk into our houses without having to see or speak to another soul, plop onto the sofa, and turn on Netflix for company. Before the advent of attached garages and air-conditioning, this wasn't even an option. People used to sit on their porches on hot summer nights and wave at their neighbors…because they actually knew who they were! Crazy, right?

Sometimes I wonder if this is why Europeans, and particularly those who live along the Mediterranean, seem to be more connected to each other and more relaxed. Europeans seem to know the value of connected relationships, often spending lots of time sitting together on restaurant patios enjoying bottles of wine over hours of conversation. For those of us who subscribe fully to an American lifestyle, we tend to champion our independence, striving to never need anyone else. Which seems more abundant to you?

Lean on Me

Perhaps we could take advice from Stephen Covey's bestselling book *The 7 Habits of Highly Effective People* and strive for interdependence over independence. Interdependence is a state of mutual dependence, somewhere between being completely independent or dependent. It is a form of connected relationship that leads to intimacy on some level.

Might the solution to loneliness be the ability to develop intimacy through interdependence and interconnectedness? Instead forgoing the development of intimacy in our relationships in favor of independent isolation without relying on anyone else, could we take a risk and develop true relationship for the sake of our own souls? If we don't connect with others, will we really protect ourselves from being hurt by anyone? I would argue that we are simply removing the middleman and directly hurting ourselves. The thought that this self-inflicted blow is somehow less painful is a lie.

As the contemporary pop musician Calvin Harris says, "Don't be afraid to catch feels." Let's connect with each other in this beautiful, messy, interconnected life—or start preparing our coffins.

Food for Thought

- Do I crave intimacy, fear it, or perhaps a mix of both at the same time?
- Do I isolate myself or make an effort to spend time in meaningful relationships?
- Do I believe this will keep me from getting hurt?
- Are my relationships fulfilling? Why or why not?
- Am I afraid to catch feels?

Selah.

Awareness Is the First Step toward Recovery

"The Lord is my shepherd, I lack nothing. He makes me lie down in green pastures, he leads me beside quiet waters, he refreshes my soul."

—Psalm 23:1–3

Change begins with awareness. After my divorce, I went to the doctor because my skin was breaking out like a teenager, my hair was falling out in clumps, and I couldn't sleep. I wanted the doctor to find out what was wrong with me and just fix it. When I arrived in her office, she asked me if I was stressed. "I don't think so." I shrugged my shoulders. She asked if I'd had any recent life changes, and I started to think. My grandma had just died, my dog had nine puppies in my two-bedroom condo, and I was going through a divorce...but I didn't *feel* stressed.

Even though I didn't feel stressed, my body sure felt it. I just hadn't brought any awareness to the fact that life circumstances were stressing me out. I didn't feel any particular anxiety at the time, so I thought my body was rebelling against me for no apparent reason. My body and mind were so disconnected that I could not allow one to help the other because I was not even aware that they had anything to do with each other. I know better now, only because I've developed awareness.

Sending an Emergency Flare

The body is often the part of ourselves that we are most accustomed to feeling and experiencing, but it's very much connected to the mind and soul. Often, our minds or souls whisper to us when they're troubled, and the body is the last to send up an emergency flare. Perhaps I may have been able to stave off my body's signs that I needed to slow down if I had paid more attention to the help my soul needed at the time and found a counselor, coach, or therapist; connected with God; or participated in meditation of some kind.

Instead, I chose to run. I ran from God, my marriage, the church, and all that I was called to be. My body continued to send up signs for help, but I ignored them. It wasn't until I was so far into the hole I'd run into that I silently cried out to God from the corner of my bed, *I still love You, God; I hope you still love me.*

I believe that was the moment that things began to change. I didn't see it at the time, but I slowly and very cautiously began to move back toward God like a previously abused dog afraid to approach its loving new owner. But God is good and gentle, and as I finally became aware of my need for help and change, God was there to give me the support I needed.

Who's Your Master?

Our current culture has cultivated expert ways to become completely unaware of both our inner and outer surroundings. Though I believe some subcultures of our society have begun to shift awareness, too many of us are still slaves to mind-numbing technologies, incessant business obligations, and distraction from the true joys of life. One of my friends jokes that the zombie apocalypse has already happened— people walking around in dazed stupors, faces slack and arms outstretched, eyes glued to their phones. I wonder if an alien race came to observe our planet, would they assume our phones were the masters and we're their genies, answering their every whim. *Buzz*, here I am. *Buzz*, your wish is my command.

Technology is a great tool when used to bring more life to the user—working remotely, more fully enjoying life, untethered from landlines, computers, or traditional offices. But when technology starts to own us, we have a problem. Jesus talked in the gospels about money becoming our master, warning that we can't serve both God and money. Naturally, some Christians have taken this verse way out of context, becoming churches full of beggars who despise money. But I believe the Bible's simply advising us to serve God while mastering our own money. Money and other earthly possessions aren't inherently bad; in fact, they're incredibly useful when they're the servant, not the master.

Knowing the difference takes awareness and self-examination. Try for a day not to answer your phone every time it buzzes. When you use the money you have saved for something important, and you feel a pang at the loss of it, remember that it is your servant, not your master, and enjoy the ability to spend wisely. Above all, look to God as your heavenly boss—the perfect boss you've always wanted—and cheerfully go about His will because He is a good boss.

When we have bosses who are kind, generous, and all-around wonderful, we naturally want to please them and do their will. But as long as our phones, friends, finances, or any other things rule our lives, our priorities will lose balance, and we will find ourselves working for very cruel and unfeeling taskmasters.

When we look to God as our great boss, we will start to see that we already have everything we need and more. Once we start believing He has our best interests at heart, we can start to practice going to Him when we don't understand parts of our lives. And that is the moment mind, body, and soul become one.

Food for Thought

- How do I develop awareness in my life?

- Am I a slave to my finances, phone, relationships, or any other thing?

- Do I believe that God is a good boss and heavenly provider of all my needs? Or have I believed God to be punishing or mean?

- How might I pray to believe differently?

Selah.

Don't Smell the Coffee!

"Each person is tempted when he is lured and enticed by his own desire."

—Matthew 5:28

Have you ever watched one of those extreme weight loss shows where the trainer goes into a person's home and starts bagging up all of the junk food, tempting sugary treats, and fattening packaged processed food that usually takes up the majority of space in their pantries and refrigerators? Why do they do this? Because temptation is always worse when it is right in front of us.

A friend of mine was once on a ten-day cleanse, which included avoiding drinking any coffee. It wasn't so hard until around day seven, when she went to Starbucks to meet a friend. Going to the place the coffee was...staring at the menu...focusing on the temptation...then buying herself a coffee. "I was just going to smell the coffee," she said. Of course, she had a few sips.

From then on, *smelling the coffee* became our code for getting close to temptation. When a friend's boyfriend wanted them to spend the night just to snuggle and avoid driving home late, we would say, "Don't smell the coffee!" Because smelling the coffee always ultimately leads to drinking the coffee. Perhaps not the first time—it may be the second time or even the hundredth time—but ultimately, placing ourselves in the proximity of temptation increases our chances of giving in to whatever it is we're supposedly trying to avoid. Do we think the coffee, the dessert, the sex, or other weakness will be worth blowing our cleanse, a little cellulite, or emotional bonding to someone we potentially know isn't right for us?

Nature vs. Nurture

When I've put myself in bad situations in the past, I think of the fable of the scorpion and the frog. In this story, the scorpion asks the frog to ride across the river on the frog's back. The frog says, "No way! You will sting me if I let you on my back." The scorpion replies that, of course, he would not sting the frog because then they would both drown in the river. Seeing the logic in this, the frog begins to swim, but about halfway across the river, he feels the paralyzing scorpion sting as he cries, "Why would you do that?" As they both sink into the river, the scorpion responds, "It's in my nature."

Riding across the river, the scorpion's stinger must have been itching to sting since the moment he hopped on. It's difficult to resist a temptation that is right in front of us or, in the scorpion's case, right beneath him. Likewise, it's in our nature to give into temptation when it's constantly right in front of us.

In my case, I think of temptation somewhat like lying down with a warm, cozy, oh so adorable wolf, then being surprised when he starts gnawing off my leg in the middle of the night. Sometimes our human desires for whatever our specific cravings—success, prestige, love, affection—lead us down paths we ultimately don't want to take.

I've heard it said, "Sin will always take you further than you wanted to go, keep you longer than you wanted to stay, and cost you more than you wanted to pay." I'll go a step further: getting close to sin will often do that, too. I can remember countless times growing up that I put myself in tempting situations that were not going to lead me any place I wanted to go.

Like sleepovers with a boyfriend because we just didn't want to leave each others' arms for a moment, especially when I was still a virgin and those innocent nights of literally just sleeping together seemed so amazing and harmless. Six, seven, or eight months later, however, sleeping included kissing; snuggling included exploring and, sooner or later, (as the youth pastors say) "spooning leads to forking." I am not saying everyone's choice is to avoid coffee, dessert, or sex. We're all on different spiritual journeys, and all of those things are good in their time and place. We need to be conscious of where these things are good and bad in our own lives and set ourselves up for success by wisely placing ourselves in positive environments and avoiding the ones that will put us in places we ultimately do not want to go.

The best way to succeed over temptation is to avoid it in the first place. But what if you've already given into temptation, maybe even time and time again? Maybe even five minutes ago? Instead of beating yourself up about it, just throw the spiritual bag of M&M's into the dumpster. Resist the temptation to run from God in those moments. We are never too guilty, dirty, or unworthy to go to God. The Bible tells us that there is no condemnation in Christ, so go to God and skip the self-blame. Go to the fountain of living water when you need to become clean. He loved us when we were all unclean, that is why He sent His Son to cleanse us for all time. This does not become a license to sin. In fact, you will probably feel like you're cheating on God when you sin, and eventually what once seemed sweetly attractive will seem sickly sweet and abhorrent, even if it never loses its temptation.

Food for Thought

- In what ways do I walk right into my temptations by "smelling the coffee?"
- What are some ways I can get the spiritual junk food out of my cupboards to stop tempting me in the weak areas of my spiritual life?
- What environments do I feel are best to live the kind of life I choose to live?

Selah.

Little Foxes

"Catch the little foxes for us, the little foxes that are ruining
the vineyards, while our vineyards are in blossom."

—Song of Solomon 2:15 (NASB)

I don't know about you, but the times I'm feeling super fit and at the
top of my game are the most dangerous times for my fitness. I start to
feel a little too sure of my health. It seems like no big deal to have a
processed snack here and a sugary dessert there—until I've suddenly
gained five pounds (okay, more like nine), or so it seems.

In reality, a series of little compromises are to blame, each
leaving us feeling a little more lethargic and out of shape, desiring to
fix it with another pint of ice cream. Song of Solomon talks about little
foxes roaming vineyards, spoiling the wonderful fruits. It is often the
little things that can be easily overlooked that spoil our good habits,
our relationships, and even our experience of the divine.

Little Choices, Big Consequences

In his LifeBook course, author and coach Jon Butcher says we will
really only make a handful of major decisions throughout our lives, but
it is the little decisions that we choose each day that make up a lifestyle,
for better or worse. Will we choose to exercise each day, to spend
quality time with our spouse, to be organized or stimulate our intellect?
He states that all these small daily choices in several areas of life are
what add up to one's quality of life.

Perhaps you feel so close to God's presence, walking in His
ways, that it feels like heaven on earth. Then the little things start to
creep in, things we hardly even notice at first. Perhaps we miss a day
of reading scripture—no big deal—then another day. Maybe next, we
watch something dark that plays in our minds for the remainder of the
week, or we decide to go somewhere that would have been best to
avoid, or we tell a joke that we wished we hadn't said. Maybe it's
something even smaller than that; perhaps it is thoughts we entertain
or people we allow ourselves to judge.

It seems sudden, but actually many little things over time bring us from that feeling of spiritual connection in God's presence to feeling far from heaven and absolutely miserable. God's presence is not far of course, but our ability to see, hear, and feel it can definitely wane as the foxes howl louder than the sound of His still, small voice.

The wonderful blessing in being alive, in the more abundant life that Jesus came to demonstrate for and give to us is that, as long as we still draw breath, we have the ability to choose. We can always choose to change directions from decisions that are destructive and choose to walk in God's ways that are always for our good. These little choices for God will be ongoing throughout our entire lives.

This is why, when someone asks me when I became a Christian, I always say I'm still becoming one every day. It's not something that just happens because we say a particular prayer. It may start there, but if we allow it, becoming like Christ will be an ongoing process that will transform our entire being until the day we meet Him face to face.

Food for Thought

- What little foxes creep into my life, leaving a destructive mess that suddenly seems out of hand?
- How can I become more aware of when I am slowly becoming spiritually lazy and out of shape?
- What are some small decisions I can choose each day to set my life in a direction I want to go?

Selah.

Habit-Forming Reflexions

"In the early morning, while it was still dark, Jesus got up, left
the house, and went away to a secluded place, and was
praying there."

—Mark 1:35

Whether or not we have jobs, school, or other duties that operate on a consistent schedule and set rhythms of routine in our lives, everyone can benefit from forming good habits. As a creative-type with an elusive work schedule, forming good habits is my ongoing struggle. Good coaching and counseling have helped me to realize, however, that routine is actually a skill to be mastered rather than just something I'm naturally terrible at and should therefore forgo attempting. That's one of the things I love so much about the contemplative church community I attend: The goal is to make quiet time with God become such an ingrained habit that it becomes a reflex, much like Jesus would retreat to secluded places to spend time with His Father in stories throughout the gospel.

The Route to Routine

In Tim Ferriss' book *Tools of Titans*, Peter Diamandis, Vice Chairman of Human Longevity Inc. health research group, says dental flossing is a correlation tied closely to our aging. It seems surprising on the surface, but he goes on to explain that people who are self-disciplined enough to floss every day are more likely to have other good habits that help them to live longer. They tend to do things like eat their daily dose of fruits and vegetables and seek consistent physical activity, and they're less likely to engage in destructive habits and behaviors.

Dr. Caroline Leaf's program "21-Day Brain Detox" shows that it takes twenty-one days to form a habit. Twenty-one days does not seem all that long... until about day fourteen (or four) of working on that new habit. What is going to push us into getting started and then following through for twenty-one days and beyond? I believe it's focusing on a strong *why*. Ask yourself, *Why is this habit that I am trying to form so important to me?*

156

As soon as I made the commitment to write this book, I went through what some have called a "dark night of the soul." Some may call it depression; others may call it necessary suffering for spiritual development, and still others may call it an attack from the enemy. Whatever it may have been, my good habits seemingly flew out the window. It was slow but sure, and there were tons of excuses. But one-by-one, my good habits (including flossing) swirled down the drain.

My habit of jump roping several times a week went first, then daily pushups, then healthy eating. During that time, my nearly 14-year-old dog died, I split with a boyfriend, I inhaled smoke from a house fire, and my stocks plummeted by nearly $30K. When I focused on all the things that I thought I was losing—the boyfriend, money, and health—the good habits just didn't seem important anymore. At the time, I had no good reason in my mind to keep them going. I didn't have a strong *why*.

But it wasn't *all* bad. It really made me evaluate where I valued my identity. Was it Christ? Or was it my relationship status, financial status, health and beauty, or the approval of others? I will admit: It was in a lot of the latter things, and I am still trying to navigate caring for my body without obsessing over being the fairest of them all. I still struggle with being a good steward of every resource and talent I have been blessed with, without measuring my worth by the dollars in my bank account or followers on social media. And I still encourage myself to trust that God has created me for connection with the right person who will come into my life at the right time, so we can do greater things together for His good.

It took some time and some wise counsel to get me back on track with good habits. But things eventually came together, and I began to feel much better as I got back into a regular routine. It wasn't the easiest thing, and I had to give myself some grace on my inconsistent routine. When I miss a morning or night of positive habits, I have learned that the whole day isn't shot and just jump back on my routine wherever I am in the moment. And if I miss a day altogether, that's fine too, as long as I get back on track the next day.

Heavenly Reflexes

> "We are both the sculptor and the sculpted, shaping ourselves
> each and every day in the image of our values."
>
> —Jon Butcher, mindfulness author and coach

Think of a time when you've kicked yourself, thinking, *Why did I say or do that? That's not how I wanted to act.* Our ingrained habits become reflexes, but the wonderful thing is that these reflexes can be reprogrammed.

In his *12 Dimensions of Mastery* program, leader Jon Butcher asks participants to identify one bad habit in their life, such as smoking, excessive drinking, overeating, or shopping beyond their means. Then he asks to identify any benefits to continuing the behavior—since our own moral compass must have convinced us there was enough benefit to keep us doing the thing we know we should not do. He continues to lead participants through the reasoning in a series of questions that lead to actions toward breaking the bad habit for good.

This reminds me of my contemplative spiritual community, who call themselves Reflexion because they aim to reflect on godly things so deeply that acting like Jesus becomes as familiar as a reflex. With time, prayer, and a bit of direction, we can rewire our brains from our unwanted reflexes toward the ones that we do want.

"Life is raw material. We are the artisans. We can sculpt our existence into something beautiful, or we can debase into ugliness. It is in our own hands." —Cathy Better, author and poet

Food for Thought

- What are my daily habits?
- Are my habits good or bad? Do I have some of both?
- What are some steps I could take for developing better habits in my life?
- What reflexes would I like to wire out and which ones would I like to wire in?
- In what ways can I pray into this?

Selah.

Part 8:
How You See Yourself

I am the first to think I'm not enough or that I must achieve some ideal of perfection in order to earn love, peace, and feeling truly at home. I am the first to forget that these things must be found and cultivated on the inside before I will ever find them *out there*. I often forget that God's gifts are just that: gifts. A gift is not earned, but given freely.

Whether it is the first or forty-thousandth time hearing the message that the best things in life are free, we often need the reminder. I also need the reminder that I am not as right or perfect as I often like to think I am and that nobody else can live up to those impossible standards of perfection. It often takes seeing my own flaws in others before I can see them in myself, as well as a reminder from God to be graceful with both myself and those around me.

Start Holding Up a Heavenly Mirror

"Let us therefore make every effort to do what leads to peace
and to mutual edification."

—Romans 14:19 (NIV)

As broken humans, our struggles with self-image often manifest in various ways for different people. Some put on false pride so others won't see their insecurities. These people come off as arrogant and unloving, but they are often hurting and afraid for anyone to see. The phrase "hurt people hurt people" comes to mind when I think of these kinds of people. Others stay small so that people won't see them and their doubts about themselves, the world around them, and even God. However, God desires us not only to shine, but to help others shine as well. This is not in a spirit of arrogance or thinking we are the best ever but in knowing that God made everything (and everyone) good.

159

What's Your Story?

The ways we view ourselves and others drastically affect how we respond to the world. The stories we tell ourselves about our worth, our circumstances, and our fellow humans will drastically affect our life experiences and the experiences of those around us. Some assume that people are out to get them; others believe there are no good partner options left in the world, while others may feel that they can't do anything right—so, why even try?

Back when I felt unworthy of love, I easily jumped to irrational conclusions. If someone I dated didn't promptly respond to my messages, I automatically assumed I did something that made them no longer want to be with me, never even considering that maybe they just happened to be busy. The crazy thing was that it took God opening my eyes (and working through a lot of trauma that I didn't even realize I still had) to see how wrong I was and what He saw in me.

Another way God showed me my own worth was in the people around me who built up and encouraged me. After being in the fitness industry for over a decade, I still struggled with a lot of body image issues. Body dysmorphia is rampant in the fitness world, and I was no exception to this terrible phenomenon. I would avoid certain foods as if they were the devil and feel guilty for missing the mark when I did consume them. It's no way to live and definitely not healthy for the mind, body, or spirit.

Then God sent me a short but healing relationship with a guy who loved my extra weight. Whenever I would eat something fattening and delicious, he would lovingly shake my thigh and say, "Eat more!" I would laugh and enjoy the seemingly sinful food with much more pleasure than I had ever known. It was finally safe to eat something that was not perfectly nutritious for my body. I would be loved anyway, even with an extra pound or two. It did not make me unhealthy to enjoy life's little pleasures alongside everyone else without holding myself to impossibly high standards. In fact, I think my eating habits may be more balanced after that relationship than ever before, and even more importantly, I learned to love myself exactly as I am. Of course, I still consume nutritious foods that make me feel great the majority of the time, but I no longer feel guilt, fear, or self-loathing around any forbidden foods.

Sometimes, we become so worried about making a mistake that we cease to live. Feeling guilty about our mistakes only causes us to hurt ourselves further. Like spiritual bulimia, we just keep bringing it back up in our guilty conscience when God has already forgiven us. Instead, perhaps we can aim for a healthy spiritual diet of all we know nourishes our souls and give ourselves some slack to enjoy even a few of those empty calories, knowing that God loves us even with a little extra chunk.

It's so much more freeing to walk through life knowing how deeply God truly loves us and sees us as beautiful, worthy, and valuable. When we can rest in the grace that God has good purposes for all of His creation, then we can seek to see the good in everyone— ourselves included. The world becomes a much richer and more enjoyable place.

Food for Thought

- What stories have I been telling myself? Are they positive or negative?
- What do I tell other people about themselves?
- How can I see myself and others in the beauty and perfection that God sees in us?
- Can I be more graceful about living and appreciate myself and others at whatever level of spiritual fitness or chunkiness we find ourselves?

Selah.

Born Worthy

"God created human beings in His own image."

—Genesis 1:27 (NLT)

I recently read a dating article about a man in search of his ideal girlfriend. He went on about all the standards of perfection he would be looking for in this perfect female and then concluded that he was not yet ready for her because he had not achieved the status of perfection in his career that would attract a girl like that. I put my hand to my head in sadness at what this world has come to.

I am all for becoming the best people we can be, all about personal development, and all for inwardly becoming that which we desire outside of ourselves. However, I want to take this moment to say **you are already worthy**. You are worthy of love and so much more **exactly as you already are**—at your current weight, age, career status, and place in your faith.

Just the Way You Are

This idea that we must make something of ourselves, by losing thirty pounds, being morally perfect, or putting fillers in our faces until we can no longer express emotions in order to be perfect or worthy is a lie. It's a lie that has become so prevalent that most of us have bought into it in some form or another. Yes, it's important to take care of our bodies, provide for ourselves and others, and make good choices, but these things do not define us. Our character defines us. As God refines our character and transforms it back into His image, He changes our eyes to see our own worthiness, as well as the worthiness of others.

It's so easy to lose sight of this as we strive to become the idols of perfection we have created in our minds. We start to believe that we have to become seemingly perfect people before becoming worthy to be loved and contribute to the world around us.

In trying to become perfect, we often lose the beautiful characteristics that truly make us that way. Our flexibility and ability to go with the flow, our trust in others, our ability to share, care, be vulnerable, and truly love all fly out the window as we look out for number one, trying to meet a standard that will probably never make us happy anyway. This perfect person we have concocted in our imaginations is never good enough, and nobody else can live up to our impossibly high standards either. We begin to lose our acceptance.

Instead of striving to become a worthy and perfect person, then find others who have fabricated similar false images, I pray we start to realize that we all already are worthy and perfect creations. There is no success, body image, or stage in life that can make us worthy. We are timeless, ageless beings that are beyond all form or title that could ever make us *better*.

Take a moment to really let that sink into your soul—not just your mind, but the depths of your heart and spirit. You are enough, others are enough, this moment is enough. We have all been made in the image of the Perfect One—all of us. Though we may forget this at times, it's no less true.

Let's choose to accept ourselves and others as we are. Of course, strive to do more, be more, live more, love more, and become all we were created for. But let's do it from a place of realization that we already are worthy and created in the image of perfection, and that is more than enough.

Food for Thought

- In what ways have I been striving to become an imaginary idol of perfection built in my mind?
- Have I built this alone or have my family background, societal influence, or emotional need to control contributed to creating this false self?
- Do I hold others to impossibly high standards? How can I be more gracious with myself and others?

Selah.

Willpower

"Rule your mind or it will rule you."

—Horace, ancient Roman poet

In the book of Luke, Jesus says that those who hear the Word of God and obey it are blessed. But what about those who have disobeyed— or worse, those who continue to disobey? Do they also receive grace? You bet!

But grace does not always take away the natural consequences of our actions. I believe that every time we mess up in life, we must remember the unlimited grace we have in Christ, but we also must learn from our mistakes whenever possible.

Coming Around the Mountain

The story of the Israelites walking around the same mountain for forty years while learning to trust God illustrates this concept well. Had they simply trusted and followed what God laid out for them, the journey would have taken a few months. By learning the underlying lessons of Scriptures, we can see where our own distrust in God's plans lies— where we tend to complain and go our own way and walk around the same mountain over and over again when we could have been in our own promised land years ago. Whether that promised land is freedom from debt, addiction, worry, or more—whatever your mountain might be—we can learn from these lessons.

Just as our culture offers a ton of freedom to eat whatever we want, we know certain results will happen if we eat pizza every day instead of fruits and vegetables. There are natural consequences to our actions, but it's important to start fresh and not allow our past actions to define our future emotions or actions.

The book of Lamentations says the Lord's mercies are new every morning. Truthfully, His mercies are new every *moment*, and it only takes a moment to decide to change for the better. Then after that moment, it takes several more moments of discipline to change that decision into a habit, which changes reality for the better.

The Weights Won't Lift Themselves

In a world filled with laziness, time-wasting, and apathetic lack of self-discipline, Jocko Willink's books *Extreme Ownership* and *Discipline Equals Freedom* have been successful because our culture craves the kind of discipline that brings about excellence. We love to see the super heroes, Olympic athletes, and superstars, but we often fail to realize how much self-discipline it took to get there and what kind of consistent habits of excellence they had to maintain day after day and year after year to achieve greatness. Just watch Beyoncé's *Homecoming* concert documentary to catch a glimpse of the hard work she put into transforming her postpartum body into performance-ready shape for her headlining Coachella show after giving birth to twins. The self-discipline is real. This is the rhythm of life: Results come after consistent effort. I believe it also comes with consistent flow and trust, which makes our effort joyful, rather than burdensome. Beyoncé knew the goal she was working so diligently toward.

Even if someone gives you a free gym membership, the weights still wouldn't lift themselves. You could have access to use whatever equipment anytime you want, but it still wouldn't guarantee results. You have to create new habits and dedicate the time and energy to go to that gym on a regular basis…and maybe even hire a trainer to learn how to use the equipment properly.

The same is true for our spiritual journey. We have an all-access pass to God's kingdom, here and now, but it takes wisdom and understanding to use that membership effectively. Access may be free, but getting the most out of it takes dedication that is well worth the results. You can decide whether you want to be like the majority of gym members who never actually use their membership or be like the very few who go and do what they can to make the most of it.

Food for Thought

- What areas of my life could use greater discipline?
- What would the result look like if I exercised self-discipline in these areas?

- Could my trust in God and the process of discipline help to create flow and joy in these efforts?

Selah.

Truly Amazing Grace

"For it is by grace you have been saved, through faith—and this is not from yourselves, it is the gift of God."

—Ephesians 2:8 (NIV)

I used to view blessing as some sort of spiritual carrot on a stick, like maybe God has not yet blessed me with the things I want because I keep messing up. What I failed to realize at the time was that God was working on the inner awareness in my spirit, getting to the root of my life rather than just the branches. If I'd received all the things I wanted before my spirit had been transformed, it may have been harmful to myself or others.

Lessons Learned

I'd really like to be married again. I was twenty years old when I first got married, and I really had no clue the kind of commitment I was vowing to keep before God and the world. And I didn't keep it. I also didn't really evaluate my potential spouse the way I should have from the start. There are many things I would have taken into consideration, and as a more mature woman I can see those things clearly. Now I would not make excuses for flaws in someone's character, nor believe they would magically change the moment we say, "I do." I know now that marrying someone for better or worse will inevitably include some good and bad traits, and it is important to know very well what those are. However, I didn't think of those things back then. All I saw was someone who wanted me (and oh, how I wanted to be wanted). And since he was also a father, I got my dream of becoming a wife and mother all at once. Or so I thought.

In the ten-plus years since my divorce, it has taken me a lot of time, therapy, and coaching to see that, although I've wanted to

166

remarry since then, it would have been disastrous for me and my prospective partners if we had. I still see areas where I know I need to grow to become more of my true self and draw closer to the purposes God has placed on my heart. And it still feels absolutely essential for me to be able to connect with another's true self.

I've seen how God has been preparing me to handle and embrace the vastness of that commitment and teaching me how to delight in people for who they are without relying on them to feel value. In these long years, I've learned to look to God and the intrinsic value He created in me since before I drew my first breath. Most of all: He reminds me that I'll never be fully satisfied by another for my happiness, instead needing to return to Him over and over to quench my thirst like the woman at the well.

Hitting the Target

I once spent a week with my best friend and her teething toddler. Most of the time, he was the sweetest, most happy and adorable baby in the entire world. As long as he was held and rocked, he was pretty content just chilling in anyone's arms. But not this trip. The poor guy was sprouting new teeth all over the place, walking for the first time, and his nap schedule was starting to change. Needless to say, we had a very unhappy baby on our hands.

Of course, this didn't make my friend love her son any less. Yes, she had to let him cry a bit to attempt to put him down for the nap he so desperately needed, and it was frustrating when we couldn't do anything to help. None of his crying, screaming, or Tylenol-fueled zombie-like behavior could possibly lessen her love for him. So, what makes us think God loves us any less when we miss the mark and act like anything less than His perfect little children?

This bull's-eye that God has given us is the ideal we strive for. But what about when we miss the mark, land somewhere along the outermost ring, or end up somewhere completely off the board? Does God give up on us because we fail? Should we? Or should we just sweep it under the rug and pretend it never happened?

Of course, we strive for the ideal to hear God's direction and obey it, but what about when we don't? Too many people simply leave

167

the archery field altogether because they haven't yet hit the target. Instead of giving up, wouldn't it be better to shake it off, try again, improve our skills, and become excellent marksmen to get rewarded with life's greatest blessings?

Growth and Change

Obedience isn't about moralistically trying to do everything perfectly and shaming ourselves and others when the arrow goes rouge. It's about graciously going back, breathing deeply, and taking aim one more time. Deciding to change, deciding to improve.

What if Peter had given up after failing to walk on water or denying he knew Jesus on the night of His death? He may never have become instrumental in building the church. Instead, he kept taking aim again and again.

Obedience forms character, but failure tenderizes the soul with humility to feel God's unconditional love. We all sin and fall short of the glory of God—not a question of *if,* but *when.* Life is about constantly returning to God, constantly returning the divine breath He breathed into us at the beginning of creation, and constantly learning how to merge flesh and spirit.

We find more abundant life when we forgive our failures and try again. There's no need to strive for that spiritual carrot on a stick; God's already planning on giving us the rewards.

Food for Thought

- Have I ever felt that God has loved me less or blessed me less because of my sins?
- In what ways has God already blessed me far beyond what I have deserved in my life?

Selah.

Part 9:
Let It Sink In

Learning all you can about a subject, becoming an expert and knowing all the answers about a given topic can be thrilling. Learning about the character of the One who created all things is no less fascinating. But most of us know that, with spirituality, it's impossible to understand all the mysteries of God. Learning only takes us so far.

Unless our learning changes us—unless we are transformed into more loving, caring, and peaceful beings than we were before—learning about spirituality does us no real good. If we are just as selfish, judgmental, and unhappy as before, then what good does learning about spirituality do? To truly study spirituality, it must become a practice. It won't be easy, but it will develop characteristics that will benefit your life and the world around you in ways beyond what you could ever hope or imagine.

Spiritual Training

"Physical training is of some value, but godliness has value
for all things, holding promise for both the present life and
the life to come."

—1 Timothy 4:8 (NIV)

Training our bodies to become stronger, more flexible, and improve endurance results in increased energy, prevention of injury, and the ability to do things with greater ease—things that would have otherwise been difficult or we would not have been able to do at all. A hike to a gorgeous mountain vista is much more enjoyable when you are not huffing and puffing all the way to the top. When your buns are burning, lungs are pounding, and eyes are seeing stars because of the effort it took to the top, it can be quite difficult to enjoy the splendor of God's majestic creation at such an elevated vantage point.

The same is true for the soul. Meditating on God's words daily, praying all the time, and loving God with all ours hearts, souls, and strength and then loving our neighbors as ourselves is like climbing a spiritual mountain. It's mind-boggling without taking the training steps necessary for our souls to grow in the faith, peace, wisdom, generosity, kindness, and love that we need to be able to accomplish it.

A New Wineskin

Just as wrong training can injure our joints and muscles, we can also walk some harmful spiritual paths that may seem magnificent at first but will ultimately lead to injury in our souls. Well-meaning spiritual trainers or places of spiritual training have injured too many people. It sincerely breaks my heart to know that so many people (including myself for a time) end up turning away from Christianity altogether because of bad experiences at churches or with church people. Such churches and people could certainly use some rehabilitation, right training, or perhaps even a complete overhaul. But church is not faith, and though it's supposed to be a place for nurturing faith, it is full of humans who are not perfect.

God still is, though. Even when we have been hurt, disappointed, or even abused by those within the church establishment, there is One higher than the church establishment, and we can always turn to Him. Do not allow bad experiences with religion to keep you from this amazing God who loves you and desires relationship with you so very much.

Jesus tells a parable that appears in three of the four gospels explaining that if new wine is poured into old wineskins, it will break them. Water bottles didn't exist in Jesus' time, so people carried sewn-up animal skins to hold wine inside. When new wine was poured into a fresh wineskin, the leather was flexible and stretched to accommodate the expansion of the alcohol. But if new wine was poured into a wineskin that was already stretched and hardened, the expansion of the wine would likely burst the skin, losing both the wine and the vessel.

I believe the idea behind this parable is what's leading to the current declining attendance in Western Christian churches. It's not

170

that society's filled with generations of heathens who refuse to seek God. In fact, I would argue that the younger generations are seeking something truer, beyond arguing theology and explaining the bullet points of what they believe and why. I believe this new generation desires to live in harmony with the earth and with each other in a way that St. Francis would have agreed with and Jesus exemplified during His life on earth.

Are today's churches flexible enough wineskins to hold this new wine? Or have our churches become rigid old wineskins that have already burst, as we unsuccessfully try to hold the pieces together while an entire generation of new wine continues to fall through?

Seeing and Hearing God

How can we be sure we are in the right spiritual training camp and not hard wineskins that are unable to contain the vastness of our new spirits? How do we know we are training our thoughts, minds, and spirits in a way that will be beneficial, without leading to injuries and setbacks for our souls? I believe that coming to God in prayer and reading His Word to familiarize us with His character are good ways to start.

Proverbs says God will light our feet and our paths. We can be doing all the right exercises, but without light, we are likely to stumble and cause ourselves injury. It's very hard to get faster and stronger with a sprained ankle. Lighting your life's oath with the God's Word and prayer is a recipe for finding truth in God. Praying before reading the Bible, praying to make right choices, praying to change matter, to heal, and to create can only cause good things both by changing the one who prays and the world around us.

I suggest you pray that God would open His Word to you, teach you what He wants you to learn, and how to apply it to your life. Learn to pray about your thoughts and to sit in silent prayer, listening to God's Spirit for guidance. His answers rarely come in the form of a deep voice booming from the heavens (but if that's what you end up hearing, right on). Most often, you will hear it in a deep peace in your heart, feeling that something is right and will ultimately lead to goodness for yourself and others.

I say this with caution, though. Sometimes past traumas in our lives can lead us to have unwarranted anxieties. If so, start praying about these traumas and anxieties, and be open to our Healer's Spirit and your intuition leading you to a therapist, coach, or wise counselor who can help you work through the traumas in a healthy and beneficial way.

Nutrition and Training

As with any training, consistency is key and will give you the best results over time. Your soul will see some pretty remarkable results after you start regularly reading the Bible with God's character in mind. If this sounds daunting, start with Proverbs. These morsels of wisdom are like a shot of wheatgrass for the soul each day, adding high amounts of nutrients and antioxidants to help you start to form a lifelong, life-giving habit.

One last word of caution when reading the Bible: It is so important to pray and ask God to reveal Himself in His living Word so that we will see all He wants us to learn and our wrong thinking will fade away. I used to read the Bible and feel so condemned in the years after my divorce. I felt like I was the sinful woman, the adulteress, and just about every other "bad" character that could be described in the Scriptures. And I've known people with mental illnesses who have felt that they were reflected in the so-called "demon-possessed" people in the Bible, as well.

When reading the Bible, always keep at the forefront of your mind that Christ did not come to condemn but to save. So, if you feel condemned by reading God's Word, put it down, and ask God to reveal the truth and beauty that was meant to come through it.

I once heard a respected spiritual mentor suggest, throughout the day when you are reading and struggling with scripture or even in times of prayer, to ask yourself: *Do I want to be thinking this?* If the answer is no, ask: *How can I think with more gratitude and beauty?* We can also apply this to our reading of scripture and to our everyday interactions with ourselves and those we love.

Reading through Scriptures with a mentor may seem foreign or challenging, but it's a great way to start asking questions and better

172

understand how the Scriptures speak directly into your life. Just as a good personal trainer tailors their program and advice to their client's particular needs and body type, a good mentor will ask good questions to lead you down paths to finding the answers your heart is truly seeking.

Food for Thought

- Have Christians, the church, or the Bible ever made me feel condemned or unworthy?
- Do I believe that Christ did not come to condemn the world? (John 3:17)
- How could rediscovering these things through prayer bring me closer to God in a new and more beautiful way?

Selah.

Just Show Up

"Bring the whole tithe into the storehouse, that there may be
food in my house. 'Test me now in this,' says the Lord
Almighty, 'and see that I will not throw open the floodgates
of heaven and pour out so much blessing that there will not
be room enough to store it.'"

—Malachi 3:10 (NIV)

My faith in God had a major growth spurt when I moved to Houston on trust in God alone. I was so broke when I first arrived that I had to borrow money from my dad just so I could keep my cell phone active for job interviews. I'll never forget that humbling, tearful conversation as I asked him to transfer the money into my account—distraught and embarrassed that I had hit such financial rock bottom. Thankfully, my dad has believed in me, even at my lowest.

Money can be an awkward subject, both in and outside of the church. This isn't a lesson in some weird prosperity gospel to convince you that donating to religious causes will somehow mysteriously bring you material wealth. It's a lesson in trusting God with one of the most difficult aspects of life: finances.

It was during my leap of faith in Texas, when I was barely holding on by a string, that I decided I would put my success in God's hands. I decided that I would be faithful to tithe ten percent of what He blessed me with as I had read in His Word. How could giving away a tenth of what I barely had in the first place lead to anything good? Well, I believed that He said it would, so I decided I would read Malachi 3:10 to myself every day. There is certainly something mysterious that happens when we follow God's ways that often seem strange and backward to us.

As I learned to be faithful to trust God with the little money I did earn, I saw Him bless my life in new and surprising ways—only one of which was financial. And over time, I went from tithing a mere $40 from my first paycheck of a whopping four hundred dollars to eventually tithing from a bonus equaling more than my year's salary. I tithed from the little I had, and God was faithful to provide the rest. He gave me free daily meals at work, a convertible to get around town, a friend who valued me so much that she cried when I was stable enough to move out on my own, and a new housemate who offered to reduce my rent to keep me around.

Humble Generosity

Matthew and Luke's gospels say that, when we are faithful with little, God will bless us with much more. As I continued to be faithful with the little He gave me, He did bless me with much more. And when my tithe on that big bonus was more than I had made in previous years, it was easy for me to give it away. Not only because I was used to always tithing ten percent of my income, but because I realized that it was God opening up the floodgates of heaven for me. Giving back His portion became sheer joy because He is the very source of both the joy and the income.

I had shown up in Texas, but the job I got when I was there was all God's. An expert in the field I was hired had warned me that the ideal candidate needed ten years of experience (I had none), thousands of dollars for licensing (I was broke), and all the right

174

connections (I knew no one). "I'll pray about it," I said, then laid the dream before God.

And so I focused on just showing up. I'd arrived in Houston with a marketing vice president title but took a low-level receptionist position at the company I wanted to work for, as I started looking for ways to help with their marketing. When a position opened up, I was the first person recommended. By the grace of God, I was able to excel in the position and live a life beyond all I had even been able to dream.

None of this would have happened if I did not allow my mind to be transformed into humble obedience. I'd moved to Texas with one career purpose in mind, only to find another much better one. God taught me discipline with my money and patience with my time, as He readied me for a job others said would forever be out of reach.

Who's in Control: You or Your Wealth?

Since then, I've taught several other people about the value of tithing. Whenever I lend someone a significant amount of money, my only condition is that we sit down and make a budget together. Oftentimes, I find the person has plenty of money to tithe, save, and pay me back if they make a few lifestyle changes. For my churchgoing friends, I always suggest including tithing in their budget. I'm never surprised when they later come to me and explain how they actually have more money left over at the end of the month than before they were tithing. And, I've also heard stories about friends who stopped tithing at some point and seemed to have less leftover even though no other factors had changed. They simply started losing their battle for control over their finances.

I'm not saying God's some magical Santa Claus who curses us when we are naughty and blesses us when we're nice. Far from it. There's no special formula for putting in a few months of hard work and faithfulness so that He will give you exactly what you wanted. Beware of anyone who preaches otherwise. Proverbs says that God has laid out straight paths for His children to live by, and when we follow them, our paths will get brighter and brighter.

As we trust God with our finances, our happiness, and every other aspect of life, we'll see He's trustworthy to take care of us. When we try to control every aspect of life and do things on our own, we often find that life can become much harder than intended. What would it look like to live in allowance and trust God with the details?

Food for Thought

- Am I generous and giving? Or are finances a source of worry and control in my life?
- What could I tithe (give to God) besides money, time, or other resources?
- What would it take to trust God's goodness, easy burden, and lightness?

Selah.

Your Presence Is a Present

"So then, let us not be like others, who are asleep, but let us be awake and sober."

—1 Thessalonians 5:6

While binge-watching episodes of Sesame Street with my best friend and her one-year-old son, we stumbled upon a funny Sesame Street parody of *The Walking Dead* that was clearly made to entertain us older viewers. In *The Walking Gingerbread*, a bad batch of cookies called Crumbies mindlessly walked around stealing other people's cookies. They slowly walked toward the cookie boxes, chanting "cooookieeees, cooookieeees" in monotone voices before snatching the boxes away and gobbling them up all up. With the slightest sound of an opening box of cookies, the Crumbies suddenly took the cookies away from Cookie Monster, eating them all right in front of him.

Upset and craving cookies, Cookie Monster faced a major dilemma: If he opened the box to get his cookies, the Crumbies would show up and eat them. Box after box, the Crumbies came and ate all of Cookie Monster's cookies, as he exclaimed, "What kind of monster would eat someone else's cooookies?!" In the end, he learned to control himself from opening more boxes of cookies by distracting

176

himself with singing and dancing, eventually teaching the Crumbies to control themselves by dancing and singing instead of eating other people's cookies. The scene ended for kids' enjoyment with a much happier ever after than its apocalyptic inspiration.

Generation Distraction

It's a silly example, but how many of us are walking zombies for the things we have not developed awareness or self-control in our own lives? Walking around with minds chanting *fooood fooood*, *seeex seeex*, or even *phooone phooone*.

So many of our addictive behaviors are really rooted in distraction and go unnoticed because we are so oblivious to any other way of functioning. They keep us from true feelings that creep up when we are not being distracted by our vices of choice that help us remain distracted, numb, and oblivious. Oftentimes, we find ourselves rummaging through the cupboards, not particularly hungry, but searching for something…not sure what, but *something*. Most of the time, that something is an emotion we are seeking to avoid, or even something we should be doing but prefer to put off. Yet, at the bottom of the box of cookies, the emotion has not been soothed and the task has not been completed.

When we become the walking distracted, we miss out on the beauty of life. I saw a photo of a young man sitting on a catamaran looking at his phone as a whale surfaced right in front of him. He did not even realize that there was life and beauty happening right before his eyes because his eyes were fixed on a screen. Screens are not all bad. They often allow us to get out of our homes and offices and get our work done in the midst of the beauty of the outside world, which is a great thing—not to mention wonderful progress for the world at large. However, when we miss the privilege of being in the beautiful world by not even noticing it because we're too busy engaging on-screen, it can become a dangerous thing.

I know that I am guilty of this myself. I am a complete photo hoarder. I look through my screen taking so many photos every day that, at any given moment, I usually have over eighty thousand photos in my phone's iCloud stream. I justify this because I want to take photos whenever I see something special or beautiful, and I just tend to find every moment special and beautiful. However, looking through the camera often leads to checking for messages, scrolling through social media, seeing how many people liked my photos, giving into my false ego self, and eventually missing out on what is going on around me. This is extra tempting when the people around me are doing the same thing. After all, if everyone's engaged in our phones, we aren't really missing anything, right? Except, perhaps, the real-life conversations that we would be having or the things around us that we otherwise would be noticing.

Have you heard of this game that some people play, where each person puts their phone in the middle of the dinner table, and whoever reaches for their phone first pays the bill? Fun idea, but I also love its purpose: being around genuine people who do not feel the need to reach for their phones. Whenever possible, let's stop being phone zombies and go back to the good old days when people talked for hours, engaged in meaningful conversations, and developed deep connections that are sadly all too rare these days. Let's be present in our lives before it's too late.

Food for Thought

- What behaviors do I seek to distract myself?
- What thoughts or emotions might come up if I decided to forgo the distractions?
- Am I running from these thoughts or emotions in some way?
- What would happen if I let those thoughts and emotions flow?

Selah.

Centering Prayer

"But his delight is in the law of the Lord, and in His law he
meditates day and night. He will be like a tree firmly planted
by streams of water, which yields fruit in its season and its
leaf does not wither; and in whatever he does, he prospers."

—Psalm 1:2–3 (NASB)

The concept of centering prayer (also known as silent prayer or
contemplative prayer) is foreign to many in the Christian faith. The
focus is less on ourselves and our requests, more on listening and
simply *being* in the presence of God. Though a pastor, a spiritual
teacher, or even a video can guide contemplative prayer, it can also be
done alone in complete silence.

The Meditative Mind

Sitting in silence can be a lot harder than we might think. In a world
where most people have too much on their plate and being busy earns
the highest of accolades, sitting still is not only difficult but often
considered lazy or inefficient. The few moments in a person's day that
are not scheduled are often punctuated by neurotic phone-checking,
and breaking this habit can prove quite challenging.

Sitting still in silence for more than a few seconds, let alone any
fraction of an hour, is something very few of us have mastered, let
alone even tried. However, studies on the effects of meditation and the
brain have shown that it does much more than simply relax and calm
us in the moment. It actually changes the structures of the brain, which
leads to greater awareness, stress management, and impulse control.
Meditation has even been shown to shrink the amygdala, which is
responsible for processing emotions such as anxiety and sadness.
Sitting in silence and becoming present is not easy, but the effort is
worth it.

Sitting in silence takes practice. A YouTube video that I often
use to help still my own monkey mind and lead me into times of
centering prayer is called *A Centering Prayer from the Christian
Contemplative Tradition* and features Rose Freerick leading viewers into

a short, mostly guided time of centering prayer where she reminds people to "pray as you can, not as you can't." She tells viewers that it is okay if the mind begins to wander during this time of focusing on God and that noticing this wandering helps to strengthen and develop the habit of returning to God. Like a muscle, the more we do this, the stronger our ability to return to God becomes.

In her *TrailerCast* podcast, my friend Elyse Snipes describes forming the habit of meditation much like trying yoga for the first time. She describes the experience of taking a first yoga class, being kind of interested because everyone is doing it and the pants are cool. The first class seems so foreign, you wonder how anyone gets into any of those poses and what language are they speaking anyway? A few classes in, you feel like you can do a great deal of those funny poses and even hold them with little discomfort. Then after some months, you're sure you're a yoga pro fluent in Sanskrit. She describes meditation much like that. Awkward at first, challenging, yet rewarding when we keep with it and find ourselves both enjoying and benefiting from the practice.

With the practice of centering prayer, we learn to return to God from our monkey minds that are often filled with thoughts about everything and nothing. When our focus on God is strengthened, then the desire and ability to pray without ceasing becomes a reality. As we take time in centering prayer to remain in His presence, with eyes closed in silence, we develop a deep sense of the divine that increases our sensitivity to notice His presence in the world around us. We open our eyes to the beauty in His creation and hear His voice in the depths of our hearts like we had never known before. We find ourselves truly living life more abundantly.

Food for Thought

- How might developing the habit of slowing down, meditation, and contemplation benefit my daily life? My prayer life? My soul?

- What does living life more abundantly mean to me?

- Try sitting in a few minutes of silence right now. How does it feel?

Selah.

Lectio Divina

"Contemplation is the highest form of activity."

—Aristotle, ancient Greek philosopher

Another form of contemplation is Lectio Divina. Lectio Devina originates from the Benedictine monastic practice of reading scripture, meditation, and prayer. This form of scripture reading is designed to draw one closer to God, treating the text as a living Word inspired by the Holy Spirit as opposed to a book to be studied and analyzed.

Savoring the Scripture

I think of Lectio Devina like a four-course fine dining experience of scripture. Fine dining establishments don't bring out large portions of food to be quickly devoured while driving to our next engagement. Rather they prepare small, intricate portions that are meant to be savored and enjoyed for the simplicity and complexities of each flavor, texture, and ingredient that the chef artistically expresses on each plate. Those who are lucky enough to enjoy a fine dining experience slow down, breathe, and enjoy small bites in order to savor the quality of what's in front of them.

Lectio Devina is enjoyed in a similar fashion. Latin for *divine reading*, Lectio Devina is a form of prayerfully reading and savoring scripture. It is not like a Bible study, where a group might read and discuss an entire chapter or more of scripture. You take a small passage, usually a couple of verses at most, and truly savor them, allowing the Holy Spirit to speak quality into a very small quantity.

Lectio Devina has four parts or movements. They are *lectio* (read), *meditatio* (meditate), *oratio* (pray), and *contemplatio* (contemplate.) Starting with lectio, you simply read the passage, pausing for a few minutes of meditatio to meditate on it and let it soak in. Entering into oratio, you pray about the passage, asking God's Spirit to open the scripture to you, teach you, and inspire you. The final contemplation phase is brought to completion by thinking about whatever was read, meditated on, and prayed for.

Inspiring Life

When choosing a passage of scripture to meditate on, it is important to know a few things about it. You may want to know the context of the scripture, the time in history it took place. What about the culture is similar to or different from your own. Who the passage was written for. The genre of writing style. Whether the story was a parable meant to teach a lesson. If it was poetry meant to invoke a feeling. Or a historical account meant to be understood literally.

A wonderful friar that I love to listen to once said contemplating the Scriptures and their meaning was the real issue of scripture—not the literalism, but its inspiration. "Would the Holy Spirit ever tell a lie? Of course not! But would the Holy Spirit tell the truth through tragedy, through rejection, through ways that are completely negative or through the agonizing complaints of the Psalmists? Of course." He went on to say that we "don't have to worry about the literal truth of some horrible things in the Scriptures, you have to worry about the inspiration of the Holy Spirit. How does that inspire life in us by negative example and positive example?"

In the divine reading of a passage of scripture, we take what knowledge we have about the context surrounding the passage and read it through the lens of what life the Holy Spirit is seeking to inspire through it. Some spiritual teachers will also ask participants to think of a gift or challenge that the passage leaves them with, giving participants something to contemplate during the week to come.

182

- Would reading scripture in smaller portions to truly savor its contents be a way of bringing the Word of God to life for me?
- How does scripture inspire life in me? How could it?

Selah.

Forgiveness Heals The Soul

The Unforgiving Debtor

"Then Peter came to him and asked, 'Lord, how often should I forgive someone who sins against me? Seven times?'

'No, not seven times,' Jesus replied, 'but seventy times seven!'

Therefore, the Kingdom of Heaven can be compared to a king who decided to bring his accounts up to date with servants who had borrowed money from him. In the process, one of his debtors was brought in who owed him millions of dollars. He couldn't pay, so his master ordered that he be sold—along with his wife, his children, and everything he owned—to pay the debt.

But the man fell down before his master and begged him 'Please, be patient with me, and I will pay it all.' Then his master was filled with pity for him, and he released him and forgave his debt.

But when the man left the king, he went to a fellow servant who owed him a few thousand dollars. He grabbed him by the throat and demanded instant payment.

His fellow servant fell down before him and begged for a little more time. 'Be patient with me, and I will pay it,' he pleaded. But his creditor wouldn't wait. He had the man arrested and put into prison until the debt could be paid in full.

When some of the other servants saw this, they were very upset. They went to the king and told him everything that had happened. Then the king called in the man he had forgiven and said, 'You evil servant! I forgave you that tremendous debt because you pleaded with me. Shouldn't you have mercy on your fellow servant, just as I had mercy on you?' The angry king sent the man to prison to be tortured until he had paid his entire debt.

That's what my heavenly Father will do to you if you refuse to forgive your brothers and sisters from your heart."

—Matthew 18:21–35

As we develop awareness and learn to contemplate, pray, and listen for the still, small voice of God, it is important to remember that none of these practices do any good if they do not change our hearts and transform us into more loving people. As we see at the end of this parable, although Jesus was very understanding with sins of weakness, He was very stern about unloving and unforgiving hearts. Sitting around contemplating Jesus' wonderful words and the greatness of the Bible means nothing if we do not allow them to transform us from the inside out. It would be like reading a cookbook full of healthy recipes but never actually making any of them, sitting on the sofa eating fast food instead.

Grace Goes a Long Way

The time that the friend I mentor came to me for advice about her boyfriend as I previously mentioned also stands out in my mind for another reason: learning to act with grace. Sometimes our past traumas cause us to look for flaws in other people in an attempt to keep from being hurt again. For better or worse, though, those who seek shall find. Sure enough, she found something about her boyfriend's past that left her so disappointed that she no longer wanted anything to do with him. I paused as she told me the information, then she waited defensively for my response. She knew I thought highly of him and often defended his actions when I believed she was acting in an effort to push him away.

Instead of defending his actions, I simply confessed to her that I had done the very same thing nearly a decade earlier that she was

184

upset at her boyfriend for doing. She was in shock. I asked her what she would do if some guy were to say that he was so disappointed in me for it that he no longer wanted anything to do with me? In this moment, she realized how she had been treating a man who had been nothing short of wonderful to her, who has learned from his mistakes and become a better man through the humility of recognizing his imperfections and allowing that awareness to change his heart.

I explained to her that, even when we do something that may have been out of character, we often hold onto the guilt and shame of that action more than anyone else ever could. Even with the understanding that God has forgiven us, it can be difficult to forgive ourselves, and we can often wonder why God even does.

In this moment, I gave my own nagging guilt to God one more time and remembered that, when we learn how much God has forgiven us, we learn to forgive ourselves, and in turn we learn to forgive those around us as well. Forgiveness is a process—not always a short one and sometimes one that requires help from outside ourselves.

"Holding onto anger is like drinking poison and expecting the other person to die."

—Buddha

Food for Thought

- Do I forgive myself for things I have done?
- Do I believe God has forgiven me?
- Do I find it easy or difficult to forgive others?
- Is there someone I need to bring into my heart and forgive now? Perhaps even myself?

Selah.

186

Part 10:
Maintaining Soul Alignment

I have the most adorable vintage convertible. Okay, it is on its way to becoming vintage. But even though it's old, it's no less adorable or fun to drive. That is, unless it's out of alignment. When a car is out of alignment it often pulls to one side or another instead of driving in a straight line. Until you go to the mechanic and have the problem fixed, you will continue to wrestle the steering wheel in order to drive where you want to go.

Such is the case with the alignment of body and soul, as well. The body may need a chiropractor, acupuncturist, or a good massage, but how do you adjust the soul? Though prayer and seeking God are long-term solutions to remaining in spiritual alignment, seeking help outside ourselves can be wise when our souls feel knocked out of place. We can hire a spiritual chiropractor or mechanic, if you will, to help us get back on track.

Listen to the Pain

"Pride leads to conflict; those who take advice are wise."

—Proverbs 13:10 (NLT)

While climbing along some jagged rocks near the harbor by her house, a friend of mine dislocated her shoulder just before I visited last summer. It seemed like no big deal at first, so she didn't feel the need to go to the doctor until the pain turned downright agonizing. Still, she was waiting for some insurance details to go through, so she put off seeing the doctor, increasing the pain even further.

Because of this pain, our regular trips to Disneyland were limited to kids' rides, and all other fun things we enjoy doing together like bike rides along the beach boardwalk were simply out of the question. A professional eventually had to set her shoulder back into position, and she had to lay off for a while before she was good as new and ready to have fun again.

When it's Time

Unhealed pains and traumas often prevent us from living our fullest and most abundant lives. Whether it's physical, emotional, or spiritual, pain alerts us when something is wrong. When pain from an injury gets worse over time instead of better, that is a good indicator that it might be time to seek professional help.

The same is true with emotions and the soul. When the emotional pain of a past trauma or ignored pain adds up, increasing in intensity and refusing going away, it's probably time to seek professional help.

Even if she knew how to do it, there's no way my friend could have set her own shoulder; the strength and angle of her other arm would not have enabled her to do it herself. She needed someone who knew what they were doing to set it for her. In the context of our souls, this outside help may come in the form of a life coach, trained counselor, professional therapist, or licensed psychologist. There are times when we must be humble and aware enough to realize that healing is beyond our own efforts and recognize when we need more than the wise counsel of a mentor and turn to the trained expertise of a professional.

Root Causes

Our bodies signal that something is wrong in many different ways. A stomachache may indicate that something ingested does not resonate well with the body, or a headache can signal dehydration. Severe pain will alert a person to treat a deep cut so they don't bleed out or get infected.

It's easy to take Tums or Tylenol for these things, but many people are dedicated to figuring out the root of the problems rather than simply masking them. Are you eating a diet that is too acidic or eating too quickly? Did you forget to drink enough water today or inhale something toxic? Many of today's health-conscious people are

188

no longer settling for the possibility of a quick-fix pill that can take away symptoms. Instead, they are looking to change behaviors, foods, and even thoughts in order to enact long-term solutions that will prevent them from seeking better living through pharmaceuticals.

Though many of us are forming diet and exercise patterns to reflect the ways we would like to feel in our bodies, many of us have not yet formed habits that would affect our souls, enabling our spirits and emotions to thrive. Of course, the body, mind, and spirit are all connected, which is why it is so important to care for all aspects of ourselves and attend to the foundations of healthy living in all areas.

This is where a professional coach, counselor, or therapist can often help identify the causes of our emotional and spiritual pains, bringing heightened awareness to the causes instead of only treating the symptoms. Bringing awareness to causes of pain will allow those causes to never go unnoticed again and will help develop an alternative way of thinking and behaving that will change the way we think, act, and ultimately feel.

Food for Thought

- Am I aware of spiritual pains in my life, or do I tend to ignore them until they become too painful to avoid?
- What are my current strategies for dealing with intense thoughts and emotions?
- Do I know the root causes of my pains, or do I prefer to ignore or numb the symptoms?
- What kind of effect might professional help bring to my life?

Selah.

Identity in Crisis

"Be anxious for nothing, but in everything, by prayer and petition, with thanksgiving, present your requests to God."

—Philippians 4:6 (BSB)

This verse is a beautiful sentiment to live by, but if we're honest, it is not something we all find possible. What happens when you pray and pray, but anxieties still haunt you? When you have begged God to take away your depression, yet it still persists? I do not believe God just wants us to live with anxiety ad depression or that He must be teaching us lessons through it.

When we look at the character of Christ, we never see Him walking up to someone, giving them leprosy and telling them, "You sure need a lesson in being humble, here you go." Absolutely not! We always see Him healing and caring for those who seek to be healed.

Certainly dark periods of our lives develop our character and teach us lessons, but just like a period at the end of a sentence, they are supposed to end. When a time of excessive sadness or worry persists for more than a season, it's worthwhile to seek some outside assistance. Sometimes a trained professional can help you identify, uncover, and heal deeper issues causing this unrest.

Sending Out an S.O.S.

It was mid-August when I broke down weeping again for seemingly no reason. It had been nearly nine months, and I had been crying almost daily. I tried to blame it on all the things that had happened throughout the year. But all of those things happened in the beginning of the year, so why was I still crying? I read several accounts of saints who experienced what they called *dark nights of the soul* and figured I could handle it. This looming darkness was just a period in life that would surely develop my character and pass leaving me better than before, I was sure of it.

Months went by, and I cherished the total dependence on God, the times of prayer in the closet and with my face to the floor before

Him. I could feel Him near in a way that is hard to explain, and I cherished each and every moment. After several months had gone by, however, I began to wonder why this dark night never seemed to end. Was there a spiritual eclipse I didn't know about?

It wasn't until I noticed myself becoming more forgetful at work and scattered in life in all categories that I decided this wasn't something I was going to pull myself out of on my own. I needed some help finding my way out. And although my temporary bout of depression in no way compares with clinically diagnosed depressive disorder, my advice is still the same. There's no shame in needing help out of a dark night of your soul. Reach out and find professional support who will listen and work with you; daylight will come, and God's mercies are new every morning.

With the help of a series of coaches, counselors, and therapists over the years, I've processed so much pain from my past that I'm now able to joyfully trust God in a way I never understood before. God doesn't want us to suffer. He blesses us with resources and modern medical miracles to help find the transformation and relief He desires for our lives.

Food for Thought

- Do I think God is punishing me for something? Why would He do that?
- Do I desire to change my thinking for the better?
- What is my current emotional state?
- Take some breaths and focus your mind to be present in it.

Selah.

Finding Help Isn't So Scary

"If we share our story with someone who responds with empathy and understanding, shame can't survive."

—Brené Brown, researcher and writer

I've been blessed to find some of the most amazing therapists, coaches, counselors, and healers to help me along my journey to wholeness. I've asked a few of them to share some advice on seeking the right professional help for each individual's needs. In all things, I highly recommend praying first, then taking into consideration the unique factors for hiring the right person for your needs. Here is their advice to you.

Tips for Finding a Therapist

Heather Beeves, LMFT, CCTP, CCSAS, DBTC
William Beeves, LMFT, CCSAS
HigherGroundFamilyTherapy.com

When you're looking for a therapist, the first thing to know is that a person should hold a license from a board that has the power to grant or revoke their license. This will tell you several things about the potential therapist right away: They'll have a graduate degree (or higher), put in thousands of hours of practical experience, and met the standards to be a minimally trained mental health professional in accordance to the standards of the state in which they are licensed. Any person in the public can contact the board in their state and inquire about any ethical complaints filed against a potential therapist.

If a person does not hold a license, then question what training this person has received that qualifies them to give professional advice, what ethical guidelines they follow, and to whom they are accountable. It is very important to consider what qualifies this person to speak into your life in a meaningful way.

Find out if they are trained in the specific issues that you are seeking help for. Therapists are required to have continuing education, but they're not required to be passionate about their training. Don't be afraid to ask questions. An eight-hour class is obviously not the same as months of training, but at the glance of a website, it could appear similar. Continued education in an area is not certification, nor does it qualify someone to be specialized in that area. Certifications generally require months of training and sometimes even years.

192

Before you start therapy, it might be helpful to take a minute and write down the specific issues that are showing up in your life. Once you know that, try to find a therapist that has been trained well enough to know how this issue usually plays out in a person's life. This therapist should be trained well enough to be able to offer you more than one solution to the problem and give you a choice in how you want to move forward. They will be able to balance having a plan with handling a detour or two without forgetting the plan.

As you start to work with a new therapist, it's very important to be able to feel comfortable in the therapeutic relationship. After all, you are investing your time, money, and emotional energy. You are the priority. A good therapist should work with you on your goals, priorities, and values—not expect you to adopt theirs.

Elyse Snipes, LMFT
ElyseSnipesTherapy.com

If you want to use insurance, ask your insurance provider for a list of therapists in your area. Cross-reference this list with Psychology Today, then cross-reference again with [the therapists'] personal websites. Narrow down your list to your top 5. Call each of them to see if anyone will offer you a free consultation, even by phone, so you can see if you are a good fit.

You can usually tell a lot by someone's website or by talking on the phone with them. It is essential to find a therapist you feel safe and comfortable with, so take your time finding the right one. Also ask friends; sometimes a word-of-mouth referral is worth its weight in gold.

Cesar Rodriguez, AMFT
South Coast Community Services

The most important part of picking a therapist is having a therapeutic relationship with them. If a therapist can provide empathy, unconditional positive regard, and congruence, that is when a client feels validated, which increases awareness. *Empathy* means the therapist has a desire to understand and appreciate the client's perspective. *Unconditional positive regard* means the therapist can offer acceptance, without judgment. *Congruence* means the therapist is willing to be transparent with the client without hiding behind a professional or personal facade. When this happens, a client feels understood, and that is when there is a therapeutic relationship.

Tips for Finding a Life Coach

Allana Pratt, Intimacy Expert
AllanaPratt.com

I recommend you choose a coach who is certified in cutting-edge transformational processes like quantum psychology, cellular memory healing, neurolinguistic programming, somatic movement healing, and more.

When looking for your own coach, read through their website and pay attention to how their information makes you feel: safe and drawn toward them or skeptical and shut down? Watch their videos, and see what happens to your heart and your body. Does it open with curiosity and feel more at ease or feel offensive like you're being manipulated? Listen to that intuition.

Read their testimonials and get a referral, if possible, from somebody who's already working with them and experiencing the kind of results you desire. You're not looking to be fixed, because you're not even broken in the first place. You're looking for someone who can help you close the gap from where you are to where you want to be and teach you skills to support yourself in the future.

Ask about conducting a complementary or discounted session before moving forward in a full coaching package, and make sure they'll be the one coaching you—not somebody else. Take them for a test drive. Do your research, Google them, listen to any interviews. But ultimately, trust your gut and your heart. See how they address your fears and concerns. Does their mentorship feel solid yet lovingly compassionate, or do they seem superior, judgmental, or pushy?

Ask them if they have a personal coach as well and why. Do they walk their talk being just as vulnerable as they are credible? I personally feel that it's out of integrity for any coach not to be coached because nobody can see their own blind spots, which is why I personally have one to three coaches at any moment.

This is going to be one of the most connected, solid, transparent, vulnerable, powerful relationships you may ever have. You will learn to be your best self and sit in the fire in this coaching relationship. It will absolutely transfer into all areas of your life physically, mentally, spiritually, vocationally, financially, socially, and romantically. Be willing to invest, knowing you will get a return on your investment in all areas when you choose an outstanding coach.

And lastly, know it's OK to be scared and get support anyways. Moving forward to do the deep work for your life to truly thrive takes both courage and humility. Yet nothing is more important than unapologetically being your best self and living a life of no regrets.

Reina Rose, Author | Speaker | Community Leader
Reina-Rose.com

When choosing a mentor, coach, or therapist, my first recommendation is to of course to pray and listen. Listen for the way God speaks to you and feel in your spirit if what is being offered is right for your current needs. Take a night to pray on it and follow the prompting of your prayers. Don't allow fear of missing out to sway you to *buy now* or be afraid to offend someone who's services aren't the right fit for you. The right person with the right offer will arrive, because when you seek you will find.

If you have enjoyed what you have been reading so far, I encourage you to visit my website. I would love to speak for your organization, church, or event, and I look forward to meeting you soon! May God bless and keep you, cause His face to shine upon you, and nourish your soul.

Food for Thought

- How might having outside guidance for my inward life prove helpful for both my inner and outer life?

- Do I have any socially conditioned biases or fears related to seeking professional guidance in my personal life? If so, how do I feel now about these biases? Were they mine to begin with?

- How could I incorporate prayer into seeking wise counsel in my life during different seasons?

Selah.

Conclusion

Soul Solutions

I believe many of the answers we seek regarding suffering, joy, and fulfillment can be found by paying soulful attention to ancient texts regarding the life and teachings of Jesus, without hurling carefully chosen verses at people to try and make them "convert." I believe learning the character of the God shines light into the dark spaces that trouble our souls, illuminating our lives and the world around us.

The Bible is mysterious and complex. The book of Proverbs is clear about the consequences of right and wrong actions, what kind of people to spend time with, and the advantages of seeking wise counsel. Christ's words, on the other hand, challenge our minds and provoke thought. Often, Jesus seems to point out just how impossible it is to perfectly live out His teachings, pointing us back to our need for the grace and salvation He gives.

Choosing Health Again and Again

As a personal trainer, I found a common dynamic across my clients. I could tell them the right ways to move for their bodies and direct them in better ways to eat, but they had to choose whether to do those things or not. Ultimately, the clients who chose to do those things increased their strength and flexibility, lost excess body fat that slowed them down, and lived healthier, more energetic lives.

The ones who chose not to follow my professional advice did not get faulty information, but their stagnation sometimes left them in worse shape than before. The ones who skipped workouts and ate unhealthy foods all the time were the ones who ultimately stopped coming back. Some would come back months later with extra pounds, lost strength and flexibility, determined to start again, while I never saw others again. The wonderful thing is that it's never too late to start over, recommit, and live a healthy lifestyle that leads to feeling great.

The same is true for the soul. It's never too late to recommit to seeking your Creator or to start learning about Him for the first time. But it's not a quick fix either. Putting in the work to help your soul thrive requires time, sacrifice, and sometimes overcoming challenges.

If you desire to choose life more abundantly, closeness with your Creator, and living the life you were created for, the time to start is now. Start taking the baby steps that you've read about here. Meditate, talk to your Creator, and know you're transforming for the better each and every day.

A Prayer from *Sacred Rhythms: The Monastic Way Every Day*

Listening with the Ear of the Heart

> *God, source of all wisdom and our ever-sustaining hope, you yearn that we, your people, would draw ever close to you. You entice us toward intimacy and friendship.*
>
> *Breathe into our hearts a yearning for divine union with you. Deepen our awareness of our hunger for you. And bring forth healing and transformation.*
>
> *We ask this, now and always. Amen.*

Reina Rose

International best-selling author and Soul Nutrition ROKU TV show host, The Soul Nutritionist Reina Rose shares her unique experience and expertise on the importance of nourishing the soul. Digging deep into the question of what truly satisfies our inner life, Reina distills ancient wisdom into practical tools useful for today's modern audiences.

As a former fitness professional and lifelong student of human behavior, Reina draws a powerful parallel between harmful food cravings and the common mindsets and behaviors that harm our souls. From stress management to meditation to prayer to mindful self-awareness, Reina's topics direct audiences on a journey toward personal and spiritual fulfillment.

Reina Rose is a successful coach and course creator. If you enjoyed this book and would like to serve your church or other organization with her help, visit her website Reina-Rose.com for more information.

Made in the USA
Monee, IL
03 December 2020

49454058R00125